Foreword by NFL Linebacker and Son **JoJo Domann**

PRO MINDSET®

Be Your Best In Your Biggest Moments

CRAIG DOMANN

Dedication

I am deeply grateful to my family for their unwavering support throughout my Pro Mindset® journey. They have believed in me during my times of distilling, experimenting and testing the Pro Mindset framework. They not only have been believers but also laboratory subjects, critics, counselors, advisors, and challenged me personally to practice what I teach and coach.

My wife, Teddi, has been my rock and a remarkable companion in navigating this Pro Mindset path. Her insights, wisdom, and professional perspective have assisted me in refining, framing, and defining the components of Pro Mindset, as well as turbo-charging Pro Mindset from a conceptual framework into a powerful intelligence that drives excellence and surpasses expectations.

I am also indebted to my daughter, Rylee, whose genuine connection to her heart has taught me invaluable lessons about awareness, consciousness and frequency. I appreciate my sons, Johansen "JoJo" and Brock, who allowed me to share and coach them in Pro Mindset principles that they applied in their sports career and in their lives. They have been beta-testers for all things Pro Mindset for many years and have given me valuable feedback on the merits, effectiveness and relevance of the Pro Mindset principles. All my children have challenged me time and time again to embody Pro Mindset on the golf course, basketball court, cycling, hiking, and in my professional life.

Our family is very close and sometimes we trigger each other in various ways, however, my family has been a priceless source of inspiration, valuable sounding board, and a constant reminder of the power of Pro Mindset. Thank you for being the pillars of strength and the driving force behind this journey.

I am immensely grateful for my NFL player clients spanning three decades. My clients' careers, challenges, successes, experiences, insights, and dedication to excellence have led me to discover, create and understand the benefits of a Performance BubbleTM. My clients have illuminated the true essence of rewriting one's story, raising their standards, and delivering exceptional performances on the grandest stages against the very best.

I thank my clients for trusting me with their dreams and allowing me to guide them on their journey.. They taught me more than they know. I share my learnings and pass on to the next class of players so their wisdom has impacted the next generation of pros.

Thank you to my parents, siblings, and many family members and friends -- you know who you are – thank you for your encouragement and listening to my stories that enabled me to reverse engineer the reasons for my clients' successes. Your support to "write that book" is appreciated.

I extend a special thanks to Lydia Weatherford, who is the spouse of Sterling, a friend of my son JoJo. Both JoJo and Sterling were teammates with the Indianapolis Colts during the 2022 preseason. Lydia challenged me to incorporate "me" into this book. She creatively intertwined my personal narrative into the overarching narrative of my Pro Mindset framework and stories. Lydia deserves acknowledgment for her superior writing proficiencies and for skillfully weaving together my Pro Mindset stories into a cohesive and captivating master narrative. Thank you, Lydia!

Finally, I'd like to express my appreciation to my friend Anthony Trucks for his support, encouragement and belief in Pro Mindset. Anthony's journey is truly inspiring—he's a former client, NFL player, and American Ninja Warrior, but above all, he's a genuine superstar in life. Coming from a foster care background, he's mastered the art of overcoming obstacles and has excelled as an author, international speaker, host of Aww Shift podcast, founder of Identity Shift coaching, and is an exceptional dad and husband. I encourage you to look him up.

Foreword by JoJo Domann

From changing my diapers to negotiating my NFL contracts, my Dad, Craig, and I have been through some shit together. Learning how to balance having my dad as my coach and now agent comes with its challenges. When we communicate, we have to clarify the role my dad is playing, "This is your agent talking," or "This is coming from your Dad." This clarity may seem small but is a monumental step in us having clear communication. I now realize I can ask for my dad or my agent, depending on who I need to talk to. My Dad played a major role in developing me as an athlete and competitor from a baby through college. By the time my dad became my official NFL agent, it felt like we'd been there before. Or maybe we've always been there. On the outside we're the first father-son agent-player in the history of the NFL. But to me, it's all I know.

Growing up, my dad's career opened opportunities for my brother, Brock, my sister, Rylee, and I to join him on business trips. We accompanied him to NFL games and training camps where we got to interact with NFL players and families on a personal level. Being around big dreams dared us to dream big. For my brother and I, we channeled our dreams through athletics playing multiple sports to eventually focus on football. While for my sister, it was channeled through dance and musical arts.

My birthday wish for every year since I was seven was to play in the NFL, and now that wish is a reality through the principles of Pro Mindset.

> " The uncommon perspective is that obstacles are not in the way, they are the way. "

Those dreams started to grow every year at the annual Pro Football Camp that my family hosts in my hometown, Colorado Springs, every summer. My dad's clients fly in from across the country to volunteer as mentors and coaches, paying it forward, back to the youth. Through the years I've heard numerous testimonies and success stories of how the players made it to the League. The common theme has been perseverance through adversity. And the uncommon perspective is that obstacles are not in the way, they are the way. Ironically, I was always most inspired by the underdog. These perceived superheroes were just people daring to be super, which I adopted in my personal journey.

I took this mindset into high school where I achieved great success winning two state titles, and Gatorade Player of the Year in my senior year. Amidst the success, my team and I fell short

> " In the heart-breaking moments (failures, disappointments, injuries) I learned to embrace the opportunity to re-build. "

of a third straight championship. Hot on a 37-game winning streak, we lost in the semifinals where I dislocated my shoulder in the third play of the game. Inevitably, after the mountain top comes the valley. My belief was tested when I was in college at Nebraska and had to ask myself, "Who am I without football?"

That question came when I tore my left ACL two times in the same year. Although my basic human function of walking was challenged, what hurt the most was the loss of identity. I then realized football is not who I am, it's what I do. In the heart-breaking moments (failures, disappointments, injuries) I learned to embrace the opportunity to re-build. Through the adversity and deep questioning, my character was being built along with my mindset.

The journey continued through more injuries, coaching changes, and losing seasons. These perceived obstacles led me straight to the NFL. After going undrafted, I signed with the Indianapolis Colts in 2022, the perfect fit for me. I got to learn from one of the best special teams coordinators in the league and Pro Bowl Long Snapper, Luke Rhodes. I had one of my biggest career highlights when I scored my first NFL touchdown on a blocked punt versus the Minnesota Vikings in December 2022.

Through my football career, I've adopted a few perspectives on adversity:

- Hardship is inevitable, choose your hard.

- The power of perspective is to accept what you can control.

- The superpower of this is surrendering to what you cannot control.

> **The superpower of this is surrendering to what you cannot control.**

My dad has helped me navigate every stage of my life: in football, in relationships and with God. He has challenged me to dream big and encouraged me to believe that I can be and do, whatever I put my mind to.

This Pro Mindset, I lived it, I grew up in it, and I've evolved with it. This perspective of ourselves in relation to everything we relate to, has guided me in creating the life I desire to live.

This mindset has guided my brother Brock, from bouncing to multiple Jucos before landing a scholarship at the University of Louisville to now the starting Quarterback for the Dresden Monarchs in Germany playing in the GFL (German Football League). For my sister, Rylee, it guided her to access her spiritual gifts which she now uses in her healing work.

I believe a Pro Mindset is being truly present and accepting ourselves as real rather than perfect. It's a framework of understanding that our life is a journey rather than a destination. A Pro Mindset uses the power of the mind to create what we really want, not what we fear. The Pro Mindset perspective will show you how powerful you are when you're clear on what you want and take aligned action.

Introduction

Growing up a farm kid from Mooney Creek, I was meant to work the soil, drive a tractor, and harvest crops. I cultivated a different path, from hayfields to football fields and from farm combines to representing athletes participating in the NFL Combine. This wasn't just a dream — it was redefining *farming* in a way only I could imagine.

My great-grandfather homesteaded the land surrounding the intersection known as "Domann Corner" – named so because a Domann owned the land on all four corners. Three of these corners were farmland, while the fourth featured a farmhouse and a small gas station/repair shop named the "Domann Oil Company," which was started by my grandfather Benjamin. My father and two of his brothers ran a family farming operation, sharing machinery, resources, and, yes, child labor.

I spent many hot summer days hauling and throwing hay bales, walking bean fields, cutting out weeds, and assisting my Uncle Bobby at Domann Oil Co. The more significant jobs almost always went to my older brother and cousins while I got stuck with the tasks nobody else wanted to do. While farming is undeniably a noble and vital profession, I often felt a sense of disconnection with my agricultural upbringing during my youth. Although I loved my people, I yearned for a bigger stage. I was fanatical about sports and dreamed of a life in the sports world. Not only did I have lots of time to dream on the farm, I would often ask my classmates about their ambitions and suggest a successful pathway to realize their dreams, too. I was not just a dreamer but also a dream coach in the making.

My journey led me to marry my like-minded wife, Teddi, and together we pursued our goals. I left the agricultural world behind and accomplished my dream of becoming a sports attorney (often referred to as a dream coach). As I represented and advocated for National Football League players, Teddi and I reared our children with the perspective that success is not mutually exclusive and that all of them could be successful in their own unique way. My wife often asked the kids, "Isn't the world big enough for all of you to be successful?" We reminded our boys both Eli and Peyton Manning were successful QBs in the NFL.

So, for the last thirty years, my story has been largely consumed by my career as a sports agent, guiding players through the complexities of the NFL and helping them realize their dreams, and as a father, guiding my children through the intricacies of life and helping them to realize their dreams, too.

Though I wasn't trying to hide behind my clients, it became evident early on that I existed in their shade. NFL front office types and colleagues didn't ask about me; they only asked about who I represented. Encounters with NFL personnel always began with "Who you got?"

My friends and family did the same thing. At family gatherings and social situations, discussions often centered around my clients. My kids looked up to my clients, so in their eyes, my cool factor depended on the cool factor of who I had signed or had drafted in the NFL Draft each year.

Brock Domann, starting QB, Dresden Monarchs in the German Football League. Photo courtesy of Joerg Meissner.

As my kids grew up, they excelled in their endeavors, achieving success as all fathers hope for their kids. I had the privilege of coaching my sons throughout their youth. From memorable games to fun road trips, these experiences were invaluable. I relished helping them strive towards their dreams, but as they gained recognition in and beyond our community, I became known as "Rylee's dad," "JoJo's dad," and "Brock's dad." I'm sure all parents have experienced this on some level.

It was flattering at first - receiving attention because of my clients and, later, because of my kids - but these conversations soon overshadowed my personal identity. I found myself more defined by the athletes I represented than by my own beliefs, passions, and self-worth. An identity crisis loomed as my sense of self started to blur.

I was living my dream, wasn't I? I wasn't in Mooney Creek anymore, doing manual labor. I had my dream job! My children were successful! So why was there a nagging sense that life somehow had more to offer?

Nevertheless, I did what I'd always done. I continued to invest in my clients' dreams, motivating them to stay disciplined, reminding them to take care of their bodies, and encouraging them to never stop believing in themselves. I helped more rookies navigate the NFL Draft evaluation process, negotiated more successful veteran contracts, and witnessed more clients gain recognition for their performance. My clients heeded my advice, took my suggestions, and furthered their career success.

But my kids ... well, my kids began challenging my advice and accusing me of hypocrisy. When I would offer them advice, no matter how sound it may be, their response would be, "Why aren't *you* doing that?" How do you respond when your doctor tells you to lose weight and the doctor is overweight himself? Naturally, you second guess a doctor's recommendation when he doesn't appear to be walking the walk. It's always easier to tell your clients and your family to do the right things. Sometimes, it takes a good mirror to recognize that you aren't doing them yourself. If you need a good mirror, rear a child.

I could have snapped back to my kids, "Do as I say, not as I do," or "Because I said so," like many parents do, but I couldn't dodge their accusations. All those lessons about accountability were finally coming back to bite me in the butt. My kids were demonstrating the lessons I'd preached – the mindsets I'd discussed so often with my clients – at a higher level than me. There was no way to avoid the truth, no matter how much resistance I may have felt about the situation.

Observing my athlete clients revel in the luxury, convenience, and prestige of the NFL lifestyle fueled my own desire for those same perks. I had set my sights on comfort, ease, and privilege, inadvertently succumbing to the allure that often leads to mediocrity and settling for adequacy. In my mind, I believed I could effortlessly shift gears at will or flip the switch whenever I wanted—but in truth, the switch proved elusive.

My temper was short, and my willpower was low. I settled for less than my best. Though I'd take a call at any hour on any day for the benefit of a client, I wouldn't keep the commitments I'd made to myself. If I didn't *need* to do something, I wouldn't do it. If I set a goal of working out for 30 minutes, I stopped after 20. When things got hard, I ducked out. When things got uncomfortable, I'd bail, or worse, react out of anger. I'd hang up on phone calls. I'd cut off drivers on the road if they did it to me first. I acted on impulse instead of with intention.

There was a large gap between who I really was and who I aimed to be, and closing that gap required that I get real with myself and take an honest look in the mirror.

This reflection got me thinking about the stories of my NFL clients – those who have succeeded beyond expectation while living a rewarding, fulfilling life and those who have crumbled under pressure and failed to take advantage of the opportunities life's given them. Those who seemed to grab hold of greatness even when life threw them curveballs, and those who walked right past greatness and never even noticed it. Some individuals are seemingly given a head start in life but fail to reach their potential, while others start with apparent disadvantages yet achieve remarkable success. In my career, I've seen a first-round draft client unexpectedly quit on the first day of training camp and multiple undrafted players (underdogs), against all odds, carve out decade-long careers in the NFL. There are those endowed with immense talent who settle for mediocrity and others with modest abilities who relentlessly hone their skills to achieve greatness.

What was the differentiator? It prompted me to question, reconsider, and refine all the life lessons I'd preached to my kids and apply them to myself. It required me to figure out what it truly takes to live those values each day. It inspired me to rediscover my own dreams and redefine what success means to me instead of hiding behind the success of those with whom I'm affiliated.

I wanted to know... What can I change or shift to be great?

Conventional wisdom, often passed on by coaches and parents, touts hard work, effort, focus, discipline, and sacrifice as the cornerstones of success. While these qualities are undeniably important, they don't entirely capture the essence of what it takes to be great. The world of professional sports is a testament to the fact that even with immense hard work and doing everything "right," success is not guaranteed. Athletes who diligently follow this advice are sometimes still overlooked, undervalued, injured, or turned away. These setbacks become the slingshot for growth for some and the destructive rock for others.

What I found is that the distinguishing factor among the slingshotted is a special mindset that propels them to greatness... a "Pro Mindset®." This Pro Mindset enables them to live out their purpose with confidence, grow stronger through adversity, and perform their best when it matters most. *Best yet, this mindset is not exclusive to just athletes. As my daughter Rylee, an artist and spiritual guide, says,*

> **"**
> Though the concept of Pro Mindset is powerfully translated through the lens of sports, it's accessible to everyone and can help us become the best version of ourselves.
> **Rylee Domann**
> Daughter, Artist and Spiritual Guide
> **"**

When I began truly living out Pro Mindset myself, I found that life *did* have more to offer, or rather, that *I* had more to offer life. I am freer and calmer. My life has been filled with intention and zeal. As this higher version of myself, I can fill the roles that once fogged my personal identity – being an agent and father – with far more authenticity and fulfillment. Thankfully so, because since 2022, I've navigated an even more challenging role as both father and agent simultaneously. It's a rare scenario, possibly unprecedented in the sports agent field, where I have the honor of representing my son, JoJo, currently with the Tennessee Titans and my son, Brock, the starting QB with the Dresden Monarchs in the German Football League.

I often start conversations with both of my sons with a clear intention: "Hey, I'm speaking as your agent now, but remember, I'm always your dad." This dual role is akin to looking through bifocals – in one view, I see the critical business aspects of professional football, while on the other view, I understand and deeply feel the personal and family aspects of an athlete's life. This dual perspective is particularly challenging during high stress situations. Advising your son-clients on the realities of pro football, explaining the intense competition and environment they are navigating – it's a complex mix of professional counsel and paternal guidance. Without the challenge from my children to reflect and pursue a higher level of personal growth, I never would have found my "Pro Mindset" that has enabled me to maneuver this new territory.

Pro Mindset embodies three concepts: Your Story, Your Standards, and Your Stage. The shaping of Pro Mindset begins with rewriting your story, raising your standards, and winning your stage. Writing yourself a new narrative will lead to more purposeful processes, which will allow you to manifest your peak performance, reach your dreams, and thrive as the person you are meant to be. Implementing Pro Mindset principles bridges the gap from your current self to your dream self. It is a conduit for personal evolution to a more conscious, purposeful, powerful, and fulfilling life.

In this book, I'll delve into the profound impact that adopting a Pro Mindset has had on my personal life, my clients, and my family, and how it has the potential to revolutionize your journey as you navigate life's rhythm, unfazed by its tune. No longer do hardships, tough moments, or daunting challenges evade my grasp. I thrive on confronting difficulties, even when success may not be immediately evident to others. It's the internal triumph I cherish, the sense of accomplishment from confronting challenges head-on rather than shying away.

To get your **free book bonuses,** you may go to this link: https://www.craigdomann.com/book-bonuses or scan the QR code below:

Contents

1. The NFL Life   1

2. Everyone Has A Story   7

3. Stand in Your Worth   18

4. Visualization   37

5. Raise Your Standard   47

6. Plug into Your Purpose   64

7. Show up   83

8. Performance Bubble   94

9. Be In the Moment   107

10. Pro Mindset: ReThink Your Reality   115

Index   123

1

The NFL Life

IN MY THIRTY-PLUS YEARS of representing more than 100 NFL Draftees, I've had a front row seat to my clients' world.

The life of an NFL player is romanticized by the media and fans: the player worked hard in high school and college and has been successful, and then he achieves his childhood dream in one shining moment (when he is selected in the NFL Draft), which precedes a happily-ever-after in athletic stardom...

Not quite.

In my role as a representative for NFL players, I've witnessed my clients achieve great success, but I've also seen them confront challenges such as unfairness, unpredictability, and deep disappointment. The NFL journey is a high-speed roller coaster. While the world congratulates players on having "made it," they are performing under the weight of roster cuts, rejection, discouragement, anxiety, scrutiny, self-sabotage, exhaustion, random drug tests, and a 100% injury risk every season. No one escapes without sustaining an injury.

My job is to help them navigate the ride.

It begins as soon as their last college football season ends. Having no time to rest, NFL Draft prospects do what they can to nurse any injuries from the season and immediately begin training for a series of high stakes showcases, including all-star games, private workouts, Pro Day, and the NFL's main event - the NFL Combine. Each event is an essential hurdle to be cleared with distinction. Each is the interview of a lifetime. The way a prospect deals with this intense scrutiny is predictive of his readiness for the professional stage. These showcases not only measure physical talents but also gauge their mental abilities to perform under immense pressure. A lackluster performance in key drills like the 40-yard dash becomes a permanent marker of one's capabilities, so preparation is critical. Therefore, from the moment the college football season ends, their training regimen monopolizes their time – planned meals, demanding recovery processes, interview preparation, position training, and multiple workouts per day – all in the hope of a positive outcome on Draft Day.

The NFL Draft is a culmination of a prospect's hard work. It is an irrevocable judgment on years of effort, which projects his potential. Athletes dream of Draft Day, and for some, it is the glorious, shining moment of celebration they'd imagined for years. For most however, it is riddled with anxiety one draft pick at a time. Family and friends gather around a television for hours, waiting for the athlete's name to be called. For undrafted prospects, the draft ends with enormous disappointment as everyone in the room - including the player - wonders, "What now?" Not being selected can lead to a mix of embarrassment, humility, and disappointment. This shattered Draft dream can trigger a crisis in confidence and belief, but there is little time to dwell on this if the player wants to succeed.

Whether drafted or signed as an undrafted free agent, the NFL journey has only just begun. Training camp is where theory meets practice, and the challenge intensifies, particularly for rookies competing against experienced older players. Unlike college where they can redshirt, rookies in the NFL must immediately justify their value and prove they are worthy of a roster spot or risk being cut. Early Draft picks usually have a more secure position on the roster, but the rest face the challenge of overcoming long odds in limited opportunities to prove their value.

Just signing an NFL contract and being on an NFL club's training camp roster may seem like cause for celebration, but the player faces an uncertain reality day-in and day-out. There are 90 players that start on training camp rosters. Only 53 players will remain. Not having a break from football in almost a year, the rookie must stay healthy and give every rep his all, or the dream could end before it even starts.

Even after securing a spot on the final 53 man active roster, players learn that there really is no such thing as "final cuts." Roster changes are frequent and can happen any day of the week. There is obviously a "53rd man," the last man standing who teeters on the edge. I have represented a couple of clients who made the final 53-man roster at the conclusion of training camp, called their loved ones and shared their success, only to get cut the very next day. Waiver claims and teammate injuries can prompt replacement. There is no disputing that rookies face a tough challenge, however veterans constantly face the threat of being replaced by younger, less expensive, and hungrier players. Each new Draft class brings in another wave of threats to a veteran player's job security. The competitive, cut-throat nature of the NFL is relentless.

This perpetual motion of roster changes is standard operating procedure in the NFL, but that doesn't diminish the real stress it puts on players. When your teammates, friends and coworkers are being replaced left and right, you can't help but wonder if you will be next. It's a fear that looms overhead constantly, and for good reason. Their place in the NFL isn't just about living out some fantasy come true; it is their job. If cut, a player is either moving across the country at a moment's notice or else facing unemployment. Real lives – not just the player's but also his significant others' – are uprooted with breaking housing leases, moving and storing possessions, and losing social relationships. Injuries, team politics, media, being away from family, and losing games heighten these already extreme stress levels.

It's no wonder the NFL is said to stand for "Not For Long." The initial excitement of playing in an NFL preseason game, the glamor of posting pictures on Instagram, and the thrill of imagining game-winning plays, can all mask the rigorous, often heartbreaking truth beneath the surface. Many players will find that their love for the game isn't as passionate as they once thought. When players truly love the game and it does not love them back, the pain, disappointment and frustration can be too much to comprehend. Reality sets in: Not everyone is cut out for the NFL life.

Every play can determine a player's future, making it a high-stakes environment where performance under pressure is key. Players, aware of the impact on their families and livelihoods, are constantly judged on their ability to handle intense situations. This creates an urgency mindset, especially for rookies who must quickly prove their value against seasoned veterans. It's a relentless world where delay in excellence isn't an option – *they can't wait to be great!*

Despite the journey being riddled with gut punches, politics, setbacks, and disappointments, many players go on to have long, successful careers in the NFL. As an agent, the process of finding, recruiting, and retaining these players is no simple feat. It requires a strong evaluation of physical abilities, injury history, and on-field production. I've been through this process, creating a detailed checklist for evaluating prospective clients, but over time, I've realized that it's not just about measurable attributes. Getting drafted may only require impressive physical skills and positive projections; however, the unyielding pressure of building an NFL career demands a much higher standard... an invincible mindset. Players who excel at the highest level must have this distinguishing factor.

Two-time Super Bowl Champion and former client Greg Scruggs emphasized on my Pro Mindset Podcast the importance of seizing the moment: "When you have an opportunity of a lifetime, you must act within the lifetime of the opportunity," a lesson he learned from highly respected strength and performance coach Loren Landow. Scruggs shared, "You have the chance to change your life, and you must do whatever it takes," noting that many fail to capitalize on such windows. In the NFL's competitive environment, each practice, each rep, is a precious opportunity not to be wasted. This mindset is crucial, as the industry is unforgiving, and opportunities are fleeting.

Scruggs's narrative serves as a stark reminder that the NFL journey is not a one-way ticket but rather a roundtrip ticket, with every unseized moment potentially leading back to where one started. Thus, the ethos of seizing every opportunity with utmost dedication becomes not just advice but a mandate for those aspiring to thrive in the NFL.

In addition to being an NFL Agent, I'm also a father of three and have coached my two sons over the years. My son Brock shared on my Pro Mindset Podcast, "Your clients were friends and heroes rolled into one. Seeing them on TV as superstars and then interacting with them as ordinary people was incredible. But what really left a mark on me was hearing their stories, understanding [the adversity each had to overcome] the grit and determination it takes to make it in the NFL. Learning that every player who secures a second contract, who makes it big, has truly earned their spot - and I mean really earned it - that was the most influential lesson for me."

The NFL journey - in all its ruthlessness - is just like regular life under hyper-speed and pressurized conditions. Benchwarmers can become stars, and starters can spiral out. Players share the perspective on time that "two weeks in the NFL feels like at least two months in real life." Wild success and heartbreaking demotion can occur in the same week. Because of this, a Pro Mindset is even more critical. The difference between those who possess it and those who do not is even more evident. High pressure tends to magnify a player's weak spots, and hyper speed reveals the outcomes rapidly unfolding. While NFL stories are therefore enlightening to the principles at play, Pro Mindset can apply to anyone's journey. In this journey we call life, we rise and we fall, and we hope to be the kind of people who can get back up again.

2

Everyone Has A Story

E VERYONE HAS A STORY they tell themselves, shaped by either self-doubt or self-belief. Your story encompasses the memories, experiences, relationships, and values that create one's sense of self. A complex matrix of your past interactions and internal dialogues, it is an evolving saga that shapes your identity and dictates your path. Your story is multifaceted, encompassing both the visible and the invisible aspects of your life. On the surface, it's the accomplishments you proudly share, the roles you play, and the dreams you vocalize. It's your billboard story or elevator pitch, the refined narrative you present to the world. However, beneath this exterior lies a deeper, more intimate narrative. This is where your inner voice, which I refer to as your "pocket voice" resides, the conversation you have with yourself and you tell yourself in defining moments of challenge, discomfort, importance, meaning, or anticipation.

Your story adapts to your life's ebb and flow. In times of success, it beams with confidence and pride. In periods of struggle, it may echo with self-doubt and reminders of past failures.

> The narrative you construct in anticipation of important moments often mirrors your current state.

The narratives you construct in anticipation of important moments, like big games or career-defining moments, often mirror your current state of mind. They reflect what you honestly believe about "who" you are and the confidence you have about your skills, competence, and readiness for what you can achieve. These narratives are also influenced by your attachment to your past and your perception of your future.

IDENTITY GAP

The Identity Gap represents the difference between our current self and our aspirational future self - the best version of ourselves. My identity gap was simply my failure to BE who I wanted to become. Our reaction to this gap can be either empowering or debilitating. This difference hinges on whether we take responsibility for our story or relinquish control.

When my children confronted my hypocrisy, I could have allowed it to wound my ego, cast myself as a victim, or have dismissed my children's perspective. However, this would have only perpetuated my existing circumstances, allowing them to shape my story. Instead, I chose to write a new story, which was key to forging a new path forward.

To rewrite my story, I first had to identify the noise that was muddling mine.

External and internal noise inhibit us from taking ownership of our story. External noise distracts us from our true purpose. It keeps us focused on the validation of others, which in turn tempts us to neglect what is truly meant for us.

NFL players deal with external noise at a level most of us can't imagine. This often comes in the form of girls and money, tempting players to buy flashy items and focus more on their image than their performance. The media plays a big role, too. Every play in a game, every rep during training camp, and – for more popular players – every update in their personal life is an opportunity for the public to offer their opinions. This can be distracting at minimum, if not incredibly discouraging depending on the feedback.

Even positive external noise must be quieted. When a rookie first makes the team, and suddenly, people from his hometown, distant family members, and any slightest acquaintance want to offer well-wishes, this newfound sphere of influence can overwhelm and distort his sense of identity.

> **Criticism can't stop them from achieving their dream, and well-wishes can't help them.**

The truth is external noise – whether it is praise or criticism – is all the same and must become peripheral for players. Criticism can't stop them from achieving their dream, and well-wishes can't help them. It is only the player's own belief in their dream that makes a difference.

Peter King interviewed then 43-year-old Tom Brady before his first season with the Tampa Bay Buccaneers. Brady shared his perspective about external noise, "Everybody's got an opinion about a lot of different things. **My opinion is the only one that matters to me.** In the end, you can either prove the critics wrong or prove them right. I have the opportunity to play, and I'm going to make the most of it, doing what I've always done. There's no room for entitlement in football. You have to earn it, no matter what you or others think or say. At the end of the day, it's about going out there and proving it. I don't put any credit into what others say."

During my journey, I realized that I had become overly focused on supporting my clients and children in pursuing their dreams while losing sight of my own aspirations. External influences muddled my sense of identity, blurring the line between who I truly wanted to be and who I believed others expected me to be. As I gained recognition for signing high-profile draftees, I pursued more rookie clients, neglecting the importance of maintaining a balanced work-life dynamic. Competing with my peers and being graded by the media based on Draft outcomes led me to equate my worth with Draft success. My purpose became entangled in shallow measures of success shaped by external opinions.

External noise can do more than distract us. When we fail to identify it for what it is – noise – and tune it out, it trespasses into our story and becomes internal noise. Internal noise is much more damaging.

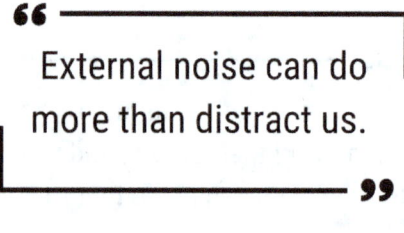

Much of our internal noise was born in moments of external noise when we were young and has been reverberating in our minds ever since. Someone told you that getting less than 100 likes on Instagram is embarrassing, and now the response to everything you post (external noise) reinforces the belief that you are insignificant (internal noise). Your parents told a family friend that your sibling is the creative one of the bunch (external noise), so your inner voice warns you against attempting anything artistic (internal noise). A teacher or coach told you you'll never be a professional athlete (external noise), so you only ever give 95% effort at practice because you don't see the point in giving your all (internal noise).

In the heat of competition, common internal noise from your pocket voice sounds like, "Here we go again" or "My bad." This noise is your deep-seated doubt surfacing in moments of failure or mistakes when you knew you didn't give your best or you should have made the play. If the seed of doubt has been watered and growing roots for years – like weeds strangling your self-belief – it can be difficult to remember who you were before doubt defiled your story.

NFL AGENT NOISE

In the realm of athlete representation, the competition is truly fierce. Unlike the unlimited number of potential patients for doctors, thousands of clients for lawyers, or millions of homeowners needing homeowner's insurance, the world of NFL representation is extremely small. With only 1,696 active NFL players and a mere 32 first-round Draft picks each year, the competition among agents is intense, as the stakes are incredibly high. We're all vying for the same limited pool of talent. This reality has often left me feeling stressed, especially during crucial final meetings where a player, alongside his parents and advisors, selects his agent from a short list of agents (the finalists).

The preparation for these final meetings is immense, requiring not just a deep understanding of the player's strengths, weaknesses, needs, and wants but also a strategic communication plan, a proven and innovative training program, and an attractive marketing approach. Any misstep, any uncertainty in my response, or any gap in offering what the player envisions could mean instant elimination. As the pool of unsigned players dwindles, the pressure mounts, and I recall the early days of my career, charged with eagerness yet haunted by the fear of being asked a question I dreaded, such as my experience with first rounders at a specific position. In those moments, my self-confidence and belief were tested. I either responded with assurance or faltered, over-explaining without truly addressing the question.

In the early days of athlete representation, I didn't fully grasp my own story. I didn't realize I even had one. It's often not until we fall short in pivotal moments that our lack of self-awareness becomes apparent. It's a hard lesson in understanding and owning who we are.

Now, I know my story. I no longer fear any questions from anyone. I can stand firmly in my values and respond with honesty, no matter the query or circumstance. There's a profound strength in knowing your story and an even greater power in living it. This journey has taught me that our story is sacred and powerful regardless of the competition, industry, or situation.

REWRITE YOUR STORY

To rewrite your story, start by identifying the external noise of your world: the naysayers, the circumstances that don't align with your goals, and the odds stacked against you, just to name a few. When other people or outside circumstances perpetuate a story that doesn't align with who you want to be, turn down the volume. This is challenging but essential because once it becomes internal noise, it's much more difficult to mute.

As for internal noise, you may not remember when the seed of doubt was first planted, but you can still kill the weed that has since sprouted. Tune into your inner dialogue and pocket voice. The only spectator that truly matters is the one inside your mind. If it's not cheering you on, set it straight. Change the conversation you have with yourself. Don't allow someone else's voice to live rent-free in your mind either.

One way to change the conversation is by reminding yourself of the positive elements of your story – your successes, strengths, and moments of triumph. Allow these chapters to inspire and motivate you.

Equally important to your story are the negative elements – the failures, rejections, and disappointments. These elements are not just setbacks; they are the chapters in which resilience and determination are forged. Grappling with this requires that we reframe our failures. Our pocket voice likes to remind us of all the times we've failed. For me, it's my career flops like the first-round Draft pick who walked out on the first day of training camp. It's the times when my anger gets the best of me like when I was coaching my son Brock and grabbed him by his hoodie so forcefully it tore. It's the times when I wasn't more attentive as a father or husband because I was too consumed with work.

Everyone has heard of Lebron James, the GOAT of professional basketball, and Tom Brady, the GOAT of professional football; however, not everyone knows that Lebron has missed more than 14,000 shots (and counting) and Brady threw 5,018 career incompletions. What truly makes them GOATs is they didn't stop taking their shots just because of misses.

> **"** You miss 100% of the shots you don't take! **"**

Failures have a way of emphasizing the gap between who you are and who you want to be. When this happens, tell yourself that you are not afraid of the gap.

That gap does not define who you are, nor does it represent a limit on who you can become. It is only a choice to make and a challenge to overcome. After all, if there is no Identity Gap, there is no dream to chase.

> **"** That gap does not define who you are, nor does it represent a limit on who you can become. **"**

Admittedly, this process is challenging. It requires vulnerability, honesty, and commitment to manage the noise around and inside of you. When your story is no longer subject to all the noise, the quiet invites you to reclaim your narrative, your identity, and your purpose.

After identifying the noise, the next step in reclaiming your story is to identify its fundamental elements: identity and purpose.

If your story is the narrative you tell yourself about your life, your identity is who you are as the main character. Regardless of who you were yesterday, claim your rightful identity as the person you were always meant to be. You are special, courageous, creative, capable, unique, compassionate, disciplined, gifted, downright awesome, loved, and most of all, worthy of being your best self. What's that person's story?

I'm willing to bet that person doesn't settle for mediocre, but rather they keep evolving upwards through all of life's circumstances. I bet they act with integrity, graciously forgive themselves and others, and inspire those around them. That they fearlessly chase down their dreams, thrive through the hard work it takes, and bounce back with even more determination each time they get knocked down.

You're that person. Reclaim it; that's your story. Discard the chapters, thoughts, and beliefs that no longer serve you. Author new ones that resonate with your best self.

When I reclaimed my narrative, I emerged with a revitalized sense of purpose. Purpose is the deeper mission of the main character (you!). It is what compels your commitment to growth to be larger than your commitment to comfort.

> **If it doesn't challenge me, it doesn't change me.**

My pocket voice reminds me, "If it doesn't challenge me, it doesn't change me."

"We have different gifts, according to the grace given to each of us. If your gift is prophesying, then prophesy in accordance with your faith; if it is serving, then serve; if it is teaching, then teach; if it is to encourage, then give encouragement; if it is giving, then give generously; if it is to lead, do it diligently; if it is to show mercy, do it cheerfully." Romans 12:6-8

Even if your purpose involves personal achievement (e.g., winning a Super Bowl), it should be revered as a sacred duty to use your God-given gifts to the best of your ability. Trust that the impact will be bigger than your own benefit. For example, when Roger Bannister broke the four-minute mile barrier, he didn't just set a world record for himself, he opened a gateway for other runners who suddenly believed they could too. We are designed to be path pavers, way makers, leaders, messengers, and an inspiration to one another.

It's easy to set a goal and then micromanage the logistics of how to get there. It's audacious and much more impactful, however, to be so laser-focused on what we're here to do and trust that God is going to provide everything we need to accomplish that mission. Beautiful and miraculous things happen when we focus on being of service to the greater mission. When we release the how, we release control, and this surrender allows us to be used in a bigger way.

I learned that true success isn't about living through others and that my identity cannot be eclipsed by their achievements. I learned that my worth cannot be measured by performance and that past failures have no hold on my potential.

> **My worth cannot be measured by performance and that past failures have no hold on my potential.**

> **A man is great not because he hasn't failed; a man is great because failure hasn't stopped him.**
> **-Confucius**

Our story is the power that shapes our reality. Changing our story changes our future. If it's a recital of limitations and doubts, it can bind us to mediocrity. We are not what we went through, and we are not the worst thing we have done. When our new story aligns with our aspirations and core values, it propels us into the highest expression of who we are. I challenge you to reclaim and rewrite your story!

I am the greatest!"
- Muhammed Ali's story

CHAPTER 2 RECAP

You must rewrite your story to bridge the gap between who you are today and who you want to be in the future.

A critical step to reclaiming your story is identifying and then reducing "noise."

- External noise distracts and discourages you from your dreams. If listened to, it can trespass on your story and become internal noise.

- Internal noise defiles your story with doubt. Reducing internal noise requires that you reframe past failures.

Your story encompasses your identity and purpose:

- Your identity is who you are as the main character of your reclaimed story.

- You identify as the person you are meant to be – your best self.

Your purpose is your deeper mission that fuels your commitment to being your best self.

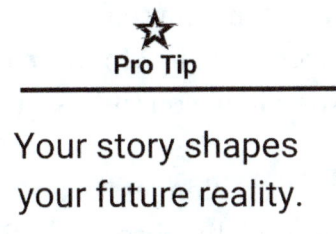

★
Pro Tip

Your story shapes
your future reality.

3

Stand in Your Worth

W HEN YOU HAVE RECLAIMED your story, adversity will soon be knocking at the door to test its strength. Your reactions to unexpected challenges and opportunities will reveal the resilience of your narrative. You're bound to fall short at times.

These tests and trials may cause you to question your story – Am I really a leader? Do I have what it takes? Do I deserve this success? Can I reconcile that relationship? Is that dream

> Am I really a leader? Do I have what it takes? Do I deserve this success?

realistic, or am I just kidding myself? Everyone else seems so far ahead of me; will I ever catch up? In these moments of doubt, it's essential to double-down on your new story and own your worth.

One of the greatest challenges I faced with my own worth is described in this real-life breakup. Being an agent often involves moments that are both harsh and humiliating, especially when you've dedicated yourself to your client's dream, only to be dismissed with the cold rationale of "it's just business." My commitment to my clients went beyond professional duties; I would attend their games, engage with their families, help them navigate obstacles, and share my vision for their professional future. Once a year, I would take each of my boys on a client trip, turning it into a unique bonding experience.

On one such trip, I took my son JoJo to Dallas to see Marion Barber III, the Cowboys' star running back, play. The game was on a Sunday night, and the following morning, we visited Marion's house. While I discussed finances, marketing, contracts, and other business matters with his mother, JoJo and Marion were engrossed in playing Madden on his living room floor. JoJo was thrilled, finding it incredibly cool to play video games with an actual NFL player.

Returning to Colorado Springs, JoJo excitedly shared his experience with his school friends, recounting the memorable trip and his encounter with Marion. However, just three days later, I received a termination letter from Marion. Shocked, I called him for an explanation. He shared that his teammate Terrell Owens had introduced him to his agent, Drew Rosenhaus, who offered him unspecified consideration to switch representatives. Marion assured me it wasn't personal, just business. While I was disappointed to lose a star NFL player, the more challenging part was the thought of explaining this to my boys. I knew they wouldn't grasp the concept that someone could dismiss me without any wrongdoing on my part. In their eyes, being fired implied that I was at fault.

It took me weeks to muster the courage to tell my sons about the situation. As expected, their reaction mirrored my fears. To them, I was the one at fault; it was incomprehensible that Marion would fire me without cause.

This threatened my own worth. My boys took his side. What did this mean? What should I have done differently? The most honest response is simply nothing. This incident underscores a broader trend in the NFL, where players often change agents multiple times throughout their careers. In rare cases, an agent's dismissal might be justified, but more often, players are swayed by other agents who exaggerate the player's market value and overpromise potential off-the-field marketing opportunities. These situations highlight the competitive and sometimes precarious nature of the agent-player relationship in professional sports, where assurances and loyalty can be fluid and influenced by lucrative promises.

Standing in and owning your worth is simply you being you (you be you). My clients who have made the smoothest transition to the NFL were the players who not only had talent but also were confident and comfortable in just being who they were instead of trying to be someone else. They "just know" they are enough, and they are.

> **Four specific identity killers knock even the best minds off their game: desperation, comparison, dishonesty, and perfectionism.**

In representing athletes, I've seen four specific identity killers with the ability to knock even the best minds off their game: desperation, comparison, dishonesty, and perfection. Those who remain unshakeable in their self-belief, however, can conquer these identity killers, and each time they rebuke an identity killer, their belief and confidence grow.

DESPERATION

When you want something so badly – whether it is for a dream to come true or for a fear to be avoided – threats to that desire can feel overwhelming. The higher the stakes, the more real the threats are perceived. This is where desperation is born. With the NFL being so cut-throat, teams often leverage players' desperation to push them towards decisions that may be best for the team but are not in the best interest of the player. With players feeling desperate to keep their jobs, they are likely to comply.

One of my clients learned this early on in his NFL journey. He was a highly talented ACC player with a stellar college career. His physical attributes were exactly what NFL teams sought, and his performance at the Senior Bowl forecasted an early-round Draft pick. However, a hamstring injury curtailed his full preparation for the NFL Combine.

We met in Indianapolis during the Combine the night before his scheduled 40-yard dash with the defensive backs. Because players can opt out of Combine tests due to injury or illness, we had an honest conversation regarding his physical condition and how it might impact his Draft stock if he ran at less than full health. I outlined the risks and rewards, especially considering the significant impact his 40-yard dash time would have on his Draft projection as a DB. He ultimately decided, and I agreed, that skipping the 40 was the wiser choice. By not running the 40 at the Combine, he could focus on the other physical tests and be more prepared for his Pro Day at his school, scheduled about three weeks later.

I cautioned him about the potential pressure and guilt from Combine officials if he opted out. My client was firm in his decision not to run and seemingly understood the pressure he would face from the Combine officials.

The following day, I was watching the DB workouts on a big screen TV from a restaurant in downtown Indianapolis. Imagine my shock when I saw my client at the starting line to run the 40. He ran two 40s, and his times were underwhelming, exactly as we expected they would be due to his injury. He'd been projected as a potential first rounder, but his subpar performance in the 40 adversely affected his Draft position, and he was selected in the third round. His decision to run injured left a lasting negative mark on his pre-draft evaluation record, with his recorded subpar speed following him throughout the rest of his career.

Choosing to run the 40 may have seemed like a confident decision, but it was a desperate decision. He knew he wouldn't run his best time on an injured leg. The confident decision would have been to trust they'd see his worth regardless of his participation. Any pressure, speculation, or even ridicule he'd face for opting out wouldn't have mattered because he could stand confidently in his story that he was a future first-rounder. Confidence would have led him to make the decision that was best for him. Instead, the pressure and high stakes caused him to second guess himself, and in his moment of truth, my client's story surrendered to his current circumstances.

Another noteworthy time of desperation in the NFL are the days leading up to final cuts at the end of training camp. Every player responds differently to the pressure of getting cut, and any negative movement on the depth chart or decrease in reps in practice signal an unfavorable indication for a player's chances. A player reaching out to his agent by phone and sharing his plight only intensifies the pressure. Only players with strong self-belief can perform their best despite their circumstances.

NFL coaches often say that they don't have to cut players because the players cut themselves. It is the overwhelming sense of desperation that causes players to make uncharacteristic mental mistakes that get them cut.

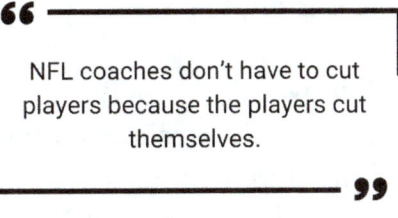

NFL coaches don't have to cut players because the players cut themselves.

Standing firm in your worth becomes exceedingly difficult when the stakes are raised, and you want it really bad. Desperation can overwhelm us and persuade us to act contrary to our identity. Two non-sports examples: (a) You're normally a patient parent, but you have been working overtime with very little sleep for three days, and your child is on your last nerve. (b) Your gut tells you to question the integrity of your company's strategy, but you're also up for a promotion, and keeping your mouth shut seems easier. In both cases, circumstances change, but your identity and worth do not. Owning this worth with consistency, even in desperate situations, will strengthen the resilience of your story.

COMPARISON

"Comparison is the thief of joy." - Theodore Roosevelt

In one of the most highly competitive environments, such as the NFL, there is no shortage of it. When my son, JoJo, signed with the Indianapolis Colts as a free agent rookie, there was one player on my radar. Sterling Weatherford, another free agent rookie linebacker, was JoJo's biggest competition in making the team. He also played in the Senior Bowl, and the media created a narrative that only JoJo or Sterling would make the final 53-man roster. I also suspected the team would likely only keep one of them. As JoJo's agent, I let him know this was the guy he had to beat.

JoJo wasn't the only one who knew about the competitor he was facing. States away, Sterling heard the same news from his agent. Sterling grew up near Indianapolis, and this "JoJo person" was going to try to take his spot on his hometown team. As articles came out analyzing the Colts' depth chart and explaining the fierce battle between the two rookies that would determine their fates, the tension grew between these strangers. Both would have to fight for their chance to realize their childhood dream.

A few days after OTAs (Offseason Team Activities) began with the veterans, Sterling (being local and having a car) offered JoJo a ride to the store. In the car, JoJo (being JoJo) randomly asked Sterling, "What are your thoughts on infinity?" One simple favor and one deep question broke the tension, and a deep conversation ensued. By the end of the car ride, they were questioning the story that everyone else had told them. "Why can only one of us make the team? Why can't we both make it?"

The rookies were required to have roommates during training camp, and – probably to the surprise of others – the competitors requested to room together. Having become fast friends, they made a secret pact to encourage, motivate, and push each other to be his best. They rejected the narrative that they had to beat out each other to succeed and cheered each other on instead.

This is a great story of both friendship and camaraderie. Circumstances pitted them against each other; the competition between them was clear. But while fans, the team, and the media compared their potential value, neither JoJo nor Sterling fell for the identity killer of comparison. JoJo hoped to get as much playing time as he could in games, and he also hoped for Sterling to get as much playing time as he could. JoJo wasn't happy when Sterling failed in practice, nor was he discouraged if Sterling did well.

Instead of comparing themselves to one another like the rest of the world was doing, they used the competition between them as motivation to propel them both to greater heights. They both celebrated when one succeeded. They encouraged each other if one had a bad day in training camp. They held each other accountable for doing extra recovery work after practice. JoJo introduced Sterling to breathwork. Sterling shared his favorite Bible verses with JoJo. Rather than believing that success for one meant the other must fail, they chose to believe in themselves and believe in their teammate and friend. Even during a high stakes competition, they bought into the idea that "we can go fast alone, but further together," African Proverb by Martha Goedert.

Contrary to surface level logic, competition does not require comparison. Comparison leads to ill will for the competitor, which creates negative energy that brings you down rather than lifts you up. Karma is a natural force of the universe, and all our actions, thoughts, and intentions create energy. If you put negative energy into the world, bad things will come back to you. Competition in the NFL is so fierce that it is difficult not to have bad karma about a teammate you are battling for a roster spot.

However, JoJo and Sterling's relationship proved there is a higher, positive energy that you can choose to walk, talk, and breathe that elevates and empowers you to be your best. JoJo and Sterling inspired each other by competing, not comparing!

Comparison can even arise in "you versus you" competitions. A poor performance can lead to hateful or discouraging thoughts. For example, your pocket voice can say in your own head, "Stupid!

You idiot! Why can't you do it?" When we think negative thoughts, the discouragement makes it more difficult to do better in the next rep. On the other end of the spectrum, a great performance can lead to pride, which is one of comparison's colleagues in identity destruction. When we have prideful thoughts, we settle for our past performance instead of motivating ourselves to strive for even better. In both situations, the comparative mindset focuses too much on the past and stunts our future growth. Being competitive with yourself, however, motivates you to keep improving.

Competition is not a threat to our worth, but comparison is. It can lead us to a false sense of being "better" or "worse" instead of focusing on the truth: You are worthy of being

> **Competition is not a threat to our worth, but comparison is.**

your best self, regardless of the performance of others or your past self.

JoJo (#57) and Sterling (#55) pictured on the sideline of the Colts preseason game (2022).

JoJo and Sterling both had successful preseasons. Their story that they both could make the team was about to come true when – minutes before the final rosters were set – the Colts claimed another player on the waiver wire and cut Sterling. Within hours the Bears picked Sterling up on waivers, and he headed to Chicago. Though JoJo and Sterling were now on separate teams, their friendship had helped each other succeed and play at a highly competitive level.

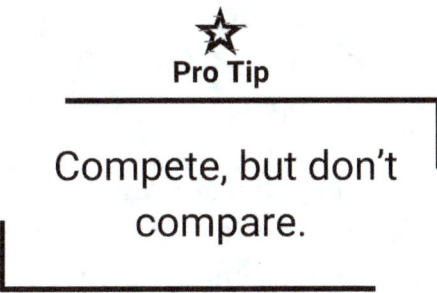

Pro Tip

Compete, but don't compare.

DISHONEST ASSESSMENT

Are you as prepared as you think you are? Are you overestimating your preparedness? Do you believe in yourself as much as you say you do? Are you as valuable to your organization as you think you are? These questions need truthful and honest answers. Many times, our reality and our perception of reality are not the same. This is a blind spot for many NFL players.

Duke Preston is a former NFL offensive lineman and current VP of Player Engagement at the Tampa Bay Buccaneers. Duke has been in his role in Player Engagement for the Bucs for nine seasons. During such time, Duke has had hundreds of interviews with Draft prospects at the NFL Combine and at All-Star games. I asked Duke on the Pro Mindset Podcast, "What is the most common stumbling block for rookies and young players that derails their careers?" His response,

"I attend the NFL Combine and speak with potential first-round picks and high Draft picks. One of the characteristics I look for is honesty and humility. I consider what happens in our world today, particularly in the social media world... you get 30 chances to take your picture to get the right lighting and perfect pose, and then you rewrite and edit the comments you add to it before getting three or four friends to give their opinion on it before you post it!

"You can pretty much create whatever persona you want to be. There's some truth in that, but it's probably the version of yourself that you wish it was rather than your reality with all your flaws. I believe I've seen a trend of guys entering the League who are so dedicated to their persona.

"Then, when you show them objective evidence that contradicts some of the perfection of their created persona, they simply reject it. Even if you tell them that two plus two equals four, they say, 'No, no, in my world, it's six.' They simply refuse to listen. All I do is present objective evidence and say, 'This is what I see, and (a) it does not match with what we want as an organization, and (b) we can help you fix that, move past that, and grow.'

"If a player looks in the mirror and says to himself, 'No way, man, that's not me.' You've got the wrong man. You can't even begin the process of growth. That's one of the more perplexing traits I've noticed in younger players recently. They would rather fail (leave and miss out on the opportunity to succeed) than refine and correct their delusional sense of self. They must admit that they do not have all the answers and seek assistance. It's a troubling trend, but I believe it's because men are unwilling to take an honest look at themselves and move past their pride."

JoJo and Duke Preston at the 2022 NFL Combine.

When you refuse to acknowledge your Identity Gap, you are less likely to make any changes. I didn't realize how my willpower had faded until I needed to flip the switch, and when I did, the light did not come on. It showed up when I wanted to keep up with my boys playing hoops in the driveway, and I didn't have the physical abilities to respond to my mental instincts. It also appeared when I went cycling on a challenging trail and couldn't sustain my energy when it got hot and difficult. I lost my second wind. I'd been fooling myself into believing that I "still had it," and was simply choosing not to use it. But the truth was: in failing to use it, I'd lost it. My story didn't align with reality, and I was dishonest with myself about the gap. Remember: a gap is nothing to fear, but it's also not something you should refuse to accept. Until I acknowledged my gap honestly, nothing was going to change.

Pro Tip

Acknowledging the Gap is the first step to change.

PERFECTION

I attended a Pro Day where an NFL Draft prospect, not one of my clients, was preparing for the Pro Agility Drill. His nerves were noticeable as he struggled to find his stance, taking an unusually long time to get ready. Once in position, he seemed frozen, unable to move. The NFL scouts, with their fingers poised on their stopwatches, were visibly annoyed at his prolonged hesitation. When he finally started, he missed touching the lines, leading to a disqualification and the need for a redo. Rather than having him go again immediately, an NFL scout advised him to relax and that he would mix in with his teammates for another try. Yet, as his turn came around again, he repeated the same drawn-out ritual, heightening the scouts' frustration as they awaited his start. Once more, he failed to complete the drill correctly. This pattern repeated for a total of five attempts. Throughout this grueling ordeal, the scouts' frustration and amusement morphed into genuine empathy, recognizing that this player's mental capacity was not aligned with the competitive performance demands of the NFL. His overemphasis on perfection sabotaged his chances; had he focused on doing his best rather than stressing about performing perfectly, he might have secured an opportunity in the NFL.

On your journey toward embracing your story, embodying your identity, and owning your worth, you'll likely find that you let yourself down more than anyone or anything else. This mental battle seems relentless. The noise will hit your ears before you can turn it down. The identity killers will speak lies to you before you can reject them, and when you listen to them, it can be a knee-jerk reaction to beat yourself up for it. "Why did I compare myself to that person?! I can't snap out of this losing streak and turn the tide! I got desperate and made the wrong decision! I'm not being my best self!"

Things work in positive feedback loops, meaning whatever seeds you plant will grow. People feel anxious about being anxious which leads to more anxiety. They doubt themselves because they keep doubting themselves. They compare themselves to someone who doesn't struggle with comparison. Their desperation leads to a wrong decision which leaves them in a more desperate situation. They beat themselves up for not performing as well in the game as they did in practice, which only leads them further away from their Pro Mindset as they spiral into the identity killer of perfection.

As you strive towards your best self, you must reject the tendency to measure yourself against perfection. As we've discussed, there is a gap between who you are and who you want to be. If there is no gap, there is nothing to chase. Therefore, the gap is nothing to fear, be ashamed of, or resist confronting.

How then, do you fully own your worth with 100% belief when you know you'll be imperfect?

As someone who preaches growth (i.e. "the Pro Mindset guy"), I couldn't shy away from vulnerability when my daughter and sons challenged me to participate in a healing ceremony. Medicinal healing ceremonies force you to drop into your heart and confront imperfections, which scare most people out of ever trying them, but once you stop resisting this confrontation and become intentional about addressing them, something really powerful happens.

My three intentions for the ceremony were to explore my identity, purpose, and prosperity. With my eyes closed and music playing, I began a conversation with God when suddenly, I saw my wife and kids crying. They were in a church with a lot of my family and friends. I tried to tell Teddi it was okay, only to look over and see myself in the casket. It's difficult to explain this experience, but through this "ego death," God showed me that the mental battle was won. I had a clean slate. I didn't need to measure myself up against an ideal or overcompensate for my weaknesses. I was perfect in my imperfections. I let go of the attachments to past failures and opened my eyes as a new man.

The experience didn't accuse, shame, or belittle me like we so often do to ourselves. Instead, it invited me to forgive and embrace my imperfections and move forward. When I asked God about my identity and purpose, He showed me that I can be whoever I want to be and can share this mindset with the world. When I asked about prosperity, the answer was immediately clear: I have everything I need already. When my sons came over to ask me how I was doing, I reached out my hand and introduced myself, "Hi, I'm Craig 2.0."

You, too, have everything you need already, and the battle is already won. You don't need to fix your imperfections to earn your worth. You are already worthy, and all you need to do is step into it.

I have fears! I have doubts! I have let myself and others down. I no longer try to hide these facts from myself or others. They are inescapable elements of the human experience.

I believe in myself with 100% certainty! I can succeed, achieve, thrive, and prosper! I am becoming my best self. I will help others, create impact, and I won't let myself or others down. This is my story, my identity, and my purpose.

Even though the above two paragraphs contradict one another, they can coexist. One illustrates the inevitability of imperfection, while the other illustrates our true worth despite our imperfection, and therefore our right to claim 100% belief in that worth. When we mix up the two, falsely believing that our imperfections dictate our worth, we have fallen for the identity killer of perfection.

Your worth is innate; wrap yourself in it. Circumstances, people, or doubts that question or "measure" your worth is only trying to diminish that which cannot be reduced, improved, or changed.

> You are worthy of being your best self, regardless of the performance of others or your past self.

You are worthy of your story, worthy of your identity, and worthy of your purpose despite your imperfections. Therefore, you are free to release your fear of any imperfections.

Wrestling with my worth has changed not only my life, but my family's dynamic. When I became more vulnerable and honest, my family became freer to communicate in that manner.

> Rebuking identity killers is the most essential game you can dominate.

When my daughter Rylee told me how I've made her feel unheard or disrespected in the past, there was an initial urge to protect myself, correct her, tell her she misunderstood the situation or misremembered, and that I didn't do anything wrong. That urge was the identity killer of perfection talking. Instead, I sat in discomfort, confronting my imperfections. I stopped resisting, and suddenly, I felt lighter. I felt free. It allowed me to hear her and respect her perspective, and our relationship has grown as a result.

Daughter Rylee, an artist and spiritual guide.

At times, failure is inevitable, and that's perfectly fine. The moment you identify the gap in your mindset that's preventing you from achieving greatness, it's crucial to dismiss the negative energy holding you back (refrain from casting negative judgments on yourself for not being or giving your best).

Embrace your narrative once more and step fully into your worth. This process will need to be repeated, so practice patience with yourself. Remember, we are all on a learning journey and we should not allow our own judgment to obstruct the lessons we are in line to learn.

Pro Tip

Identifying and rebuking identity killers is the most essential game you can dominate. You're learning to speak to yourself with respect, crafting mental sanctuaries, and believing in yourself 100% despite your circumstances.

Stepping into our worth helps us grapple with the unceasing adversity of life. We can't control what happens. We can't control whether we make the team, or even whether we score the next point. Perfection is impossible. But we can control how we respond or react. There is power and peace in embracing your imperfection.

This is more than self-discovery. It is a practice of self-mastery that unlocks your boundless potential. You are not just sweeping away mental debris; you are erecting a launchpad for exponential growth as you align with your purpose, claim your worthiness, and sharpen your mental edge.

CHAPTER 3 RECAP

Your reaction to adversity will test the strength of your story. Standing in your worth requires that you rebuke identity killers. *The four identity killers are:*

1. Desperation
- High stakes and added pressure increase the difficulty of making decisions that align with your story.

- Know the difference between confident decisions and desperate decisions.

2. Comparison
- We can compare or compete against others or against our own past performances.

- Comparison creates destructive energy, while competition motivates us to be the best version of ourselves.

3. Dishonest Assessment
- Honestly assess your strengths, weaknesses, skills, and abilities.

- Identify your Identity Gap.

- Redefine and redesign your sense of self.

4. Perfection
- Perfection is impossible.

- Confronting our imperfections can be scary, but releasing the fear of them empowers us to own our worth.

Pro Tip

You have to rebuke these identity killers perpetually and often, so be patient with yourself.

4

Visualization

THE FIRST FOUNDATIONAL ELEMENT of Pro Mindset is your Story. Your story is the narrative you tell yourself, which encompasses your identity and your purpose. The second element, Standards, is what level of commitment and sacrifice are you willing to pay to accomplish your dreams. What do I need to do to achieve my dreams?

Muhammed Ali is credited with the quote, "If my mind can conceive it and my heart can believe it – then I can achieve it," but variations of this quote have been used throughout history,

> "
> If my mind can conceive it
> and my heart can believe it –
> then I can achieve it.
> "

and for good reason! We've already explored the importance of belief, which is the foundation of your story. Hopefully, your heart is beginning to believe it. What's left, then, is getting your mind to conceive it.

Our brains switch between thinking about the past, present, and future. Remembering the past may be helpful in terms of personal reflection, but – as we've discussed – lingering too long can be largely unhelpful as it takes you away from the present. Undoubtedly, being present has huge benefits in terms of both performance and joy (We will dive into this more deeply later). But to conceive that which hasn't yet occurred, we must imagine the future. Visualization is a powerful tool for mentally rehearsing desired outcomes, enhancing performance, and achieving dreams by creating vivid, emotionally engaging mental scenarios.

My sons, JoJo and Brock (2022), at Domann Oil Co. on Domann Corner in Mooney Creek

One of my least favorite jobs growing up in Mooney Creek was sitting atop Uncle Bobby's gas truck, filling up the delivery tanks from his storage tanks. The absence of an automatic shutoff mechanism meant I had to manually handle the gas hose nozzle, check fuel levels to prevent overflows, and wait tediously to switch it between the three tanks on his medium-sized gas truck. There wasn't anything to distract me from the summer heat, the smell of the gas fumes, or the bubbling energy inherent to being a teen boy, which was held hostage by the absolute monotony of the task. To deal with my sheer boredom and discomfort, my mind would wander to a more purposeful future.

As a kid enthralled with sports, my mind dreamt up exciting games wherein my strategic plays and athletic movements would end in successful outcomes. I might imagine that I'm George Brett, a baseball player for the Kansas City Royals at that time. I'd be at the plate, three and two count, and I'd hear the crowd. Then, as the ball connected with my bat, I'd feel the confidence of being that clutch performer flow through me. I'd imagine the upcoming football season, playing out the intricacies of different calls in my head. The ball would spin off my hand perfectly, flying to the exact spot where it would be secured by the intended receiver.

All my daydreaming did not go to waste. In fact, I was unconsciously employing a tool known as visualization. By visualizing myself and my team succeeding, I was increasing my likelihood of success. Each daydream was a mental rep, as I practiced strategy, movements, and confidence under pressure, all within the simulation of my mind.

I'd complete a pass before I threw it. I'd hit a home run before I stepped up to the plate. I'd not only see myself as the star, but also see how I would put my teammates in optimal positions to succeed. This is probably why my high school football coach entrusted me as the starting QB to call the plays for three years. My team went to the Kansas 4A State Championship during my senior season, but I'd already been there 100 times and won every time.

When you attempt something challenging, whether it be a game, interview, negotiation conversation, or just another busy day, taking the time to visualize success puts the authorship of your story back in your hands. It will not go exactly as you imagine, but it gives you a game plan and more importantly, a success-oriented mindset.

As the QB coach for Pine Creek High School, the reigning State Champs riding a 12-game winning streak, I was coaching on the sidelines during a game versus our archrival. As the game clock ticked under five minutes, the scoreboard read 21-20 against us. Our spectators braced for what seemed like an inevitable upset. Our opponent had the ball and was steadily moving down the field. The scenarios seemed clear: either our opponent would score a touchdown, leaving us with little time to retaliate, or they would turn the ball over on downs deep in our territory, effectively ending our chances.

However, an unorthodox strategy crystallized in my mind that I had mentally played out just for this occasion. What if we let them score? This idea, seemingly counterintuitive, played out like a chess match in my head. By allowing them to score, we could gain control of the clock and our destiny, giving us more than two minutes to drive down the field, score a touchdown and a 2-point conversion, and push the game into overtime. It was a strategic concession: a momentary step back for a potential greater advance.

I presented this idea to our head coach, who, despite initial skepticism, made the bold call. Our unsuspecting opponent scored on a subsequent 20+ yard run, and their extra point put them eight points ahead with just over two minutes left. The stage was set for a thrilling finish.

Brock, Teddi, JoJo and me after a Pine Creek H.S. game (2015).

Our offense advanced down the field with urgency, scored a touchdown and nailed the 2-point conversion. Tied at 28-28 with seconds to spare, we headed into overtime. Our eventual 34-28 win in overtime left our opponents in disbelief. After this come-from-behind victory, Pine Creek went on a 37-game winning streak!

Scoreboards are explicit in sports, but they're often invisible, indefinite, and ambiguous in life. In both cases, you can visualize and anticipate various scenarios for success. Sometimes, the best action is not necessarily linear. Sometimes we must take a step backwards in order to take a bigger step forward in the strongest manner.

GAME MVP IN THE FIRST START

My son Brock's journey to his first D1 Power 5 start for Louisville against Virginia in Charlottesville during the 2022 season was a testament to his visualization and perseverance. I witnessed him stepping into his long-awaited dream, a dream he had relentlessly pursued despite numerous challenges, skeptics, and critics. For Brock, the game had already been played countless times in his mind. Even when Louisville fell behind early in the game, Brock remained unshaken – neither the harsh words from his coach nor the building momentum of Virginia could deter him. This was more than a game; it was the realization of his dream.

The game's pivotal moment unfolded in the first half during a critical 4th and 2 situation, with Louisville trailing 10-3. The team desperately needed a boost, and the Head Coach's call for a run play seemed like a straightforward decision. Brock, poised to hand off to his running back, encountered a familiar scenario he had visualized many times. Noticing the defensive end crashing down to disrupt the play, Brock made a split-second decision. Instead of the planned handoff, he kept the ball and dashed 44 yards for a touchdown, flipping the game's momentum on its head. It was a play that showcased not just his awareness and instincts but also his ability to adapt swiftly to changing dynamics on the field.

Brock's decision to deviate from the planned play underlined his acute situational awareness and mental rehearsals. When he saw the defensive end closing in, his decision to run with the ball was not just a testament to his physical abilities but also his mental agility and game intelligence. It was a moment that defined the game, a reflection of Brock's journey – one where resilience, adaptability, and a deep belief in his dream merged to create a memorable victory for Louisville. Brock was named MVP of the game.

1ST NFL TOUCHDOWN

My son JoJo (#57) with the Indianapolis Colts scored his first NFL touchdown against the Vikings on a blocked punt returned for a touchdown. JoJo told me afterwards that he dreamed of this touchdown play the week of the game. When the ball was in the air, everything slowed down as he caught the ball before running into the end zone. It happened exactly how he visualized it.

Without visualizing success, you're entirely reactive to the circumstances. Being on your heels is a well-known mistake for any athlete. If things take a wrong turn, you might end up labeling yourself as the loser in that scenario.

> " Victorious warriors win first and then go to war, while defeated warriors go to war first and then seek to win. "

With visualization, you've already won. You're on your toes, attacking the challenge proactively. If something goes wrong, the confidence of having won already in your mind allows you to jump the hurdle with the certainty that you'll land on your feet and come out on top. As Sun Tzu says in <u>The Art of War</u>, "Victorious warriors win first and then go to war, while defeated warriors go to war first and then seek to win."

"Every battle is won before it is fought" is the version quoted by former Patriots' longtime head coach, Bill Belichick.

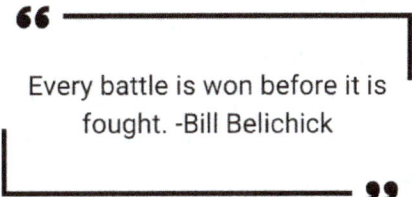

> Every battle is won before it is fought. -Bill Belichick

Many successful athletes practice visualization. I interviewed Bob Tewksbury, former Major League Pitcher, on an episode of Pro Mindset Podcast and he shared his practice, which started back in high school. "I started to use imagery to see myself perform. I would just put on some music, close my eyes, and imagine myself pitching. [...] It was really powerful."

His blueprint for success didn't change when he got his shot to make it to the big leagues and went to Fort Lauderdale for Spring Training with the Yankees. Instead of simply hoping to make the team, he conjured up a vivid image of himself walking into manager Lou Piniella's office and being told that he made the team. "I created this image so powerful that I would cry" shared Tewksbury.

Bob would wake up on his pitching day, and he'd go out to the beach, listen to music just like back in high school, freely and loosely dance around, and imagine himself pitching against the day's opponent. He pitched 40 consecutive, scoreless innings that Spring. With a week left in spring training, he was tapped on the shoulder by someone who said, "Hey, Lou wants to see you." He strolled across the big New York Yankees logo in the locker room, entered Lou's office, and literally walked into his dream.

Bob went on to have a successful career, claiming the second-lowest base on balls per inning ratio since the 1920s. "I practiced [visualization] my whole career and I have games that I won even before I ever threw a pitch."

Harnessing the power of visualization proves undeniably potent in raising your standards. The clearer your vision of the future, the more seamless the process of aligning your standards with your dreams becomes.

Visualization, positive or negative, is likely something you have utilized or experienced. Have you ever let your mind wander during a hot shower only to find yourself imagining your worst fear happening in such vivid detail you wish you could turn it off? Or thinking meticulously about how your Plan B could play out instead of your Plan A? Intentional positive visualization manifests your dreams, but haphazard visualization can amplify negative feelings, allow fear to supersede faith, and manifest mediocrity.

Shutting down these invasive images is much like the practice of rebuking identity killers – repetitive and mental.

> **"** Taking the time to purposefully visualize can help reprogram your subconscious by tipping the scale in the positive direction. **"**

Taking the time to purposefully visualize can help reprogram your subconscious by tipping the scale in the positive direction.

One simple way to tip the imagery scale is by using highlight reels. When I was juggling work, family, and youth coaching responsibilities, I spent plane rides watching game tapes, and making individual highlight reels for JoJo and Brock. Even though one game might only have a few highlight plays, compiling them over several games created a substantial collection.

They were captivated by their highlights, watching them repeatedly. They began making their own, sometimes revisiting plays as far back as the 6th grade. Watching themselves excel on the field, even in small doses, began to instill a belief in their subconscious that they were capable of greatness. I witnessed something incredible happen: the more they watched, the more they believed, and the better they performed. With each improved performance, their confidence soared to new heights.

This visualization practice is a strategic way to revisit and relive past moments of greatness. Most of us don't have a literal highlight reel, but there are certainly times

> **"** Purposeful visualization helps reprogram your subconscious. **"**

in our past when we acted or performed in accordance with our best self. Remembering these moments – recalling the confidence, grace, intuition, and skill with which you acted – is a great starting point to visualize a future wherein you experience this same euphoric feeling of achievement. Highlight reels reinforce the belief in your story. You can make plays, be a star, and rise to the occasion. You already have!

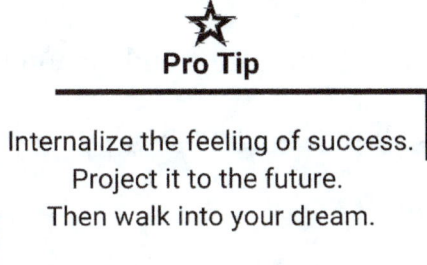

★
Pro Tip

Internalize the feeling of success.
Project it to the future.
Then walk into your dream.

CHAPTER 4 RECAP

Believing in what you envision is key to achieving your goals.

The act of mentally picturing success, known as visualization, is a potent technique often employed by top athletes as part of their performance systems.

Dedicating time to visualize future triumphs empowers you to take control of your narrative.

Visualization effectively reprograms your subconscious mind.

By imagining various successful outcomes, what may appear as a step back to others is actually a strategic move forward in your journey.

Reflecting on your past achievements and creating your own highlight reels, assists in envisioning future successes.

Visualization enhances several key aspects:
- Heightened situational awareness

- Better understanding of the game's pace

- Improved problem-solving and identification of solutions

- Navigating through challenging situations toward success

5

Raise Your Standard

"A goal is a dream with a plan and a deadline." –
Harvey Mackay.

WITHIN THE CHRISTIAN RELIGION, there is an age-old discussion about the relationship between faith and works. Good works are not what saves us, Biblical Christians would agree, but still, "Faith by itself, if it is not accompanied by action, is dead" (James 2:17-23). In the same way, building belief in your story is only meaningful if you allow this belief to influence your actions.

> Belief is fundamental, but we cannot expect to simply believe our way into greatness.

Belief is fundamental, but we cannot expect to simply believe our way into greatness. We must allow our beliefs to drive our actions, and our actions must reinforce our beliefs. For example, if you identify as an artist, your belief in this identity would drive you to make art, and each minute spent creating would reinforce your belief that you are, in fact, an artist.

Our story builds and is supported by our standards and systems, which consist of our habits, routines, and focused training. Typically, our parents lay the foundation for these systems, instilling in us the significance of preparation, consistent sleep schedules, healthy eating, punctuality, and hard work. As you progress to high school, coaches further develop these systems, emphasizing strength, speed, and skill training.

Every NFL player lifts, trains, prepares, works hard, studies his playbook, and watches film of his upcoming opponent. However, the true distinction between success and failure isn't just about doing these activities. Rather, it's about the higher standard a player brings and commits to every single day.

In the NFL, players take their systems to extraordinary heights. I call them "High Performance Training Systems." With their career depending on their bodies, they must embody their identity as a professional athlete in everything they do. When they work out, there is no such thing as "just a quick pump." Each rep must be executed with exceptional form. Food is more than sustenance; it's nourishment and fuel for their bodies to heal and perform at their highest level. So many players avoid processed foods, source locally, take NFL-approved supplements, or consult with nutritionists to perfect their macronutrient ratio intake. Recovery is of utmost importance; players can't skate by with a quick warmup before practice. They come into work early and spend hours in the evening just to stay healthy, subjecting themselves to cold plunging, grastoning out scar tissue, getting needled, yoga, ARP therapy to correct compensation patterns, or physical therapy to maintain top physical condition. They go beyond getting eight hours of sleep: they turn off their devices and any bright lights hours before bed, they spike their melatonin production by drinking tart cherry juice, and they invest in the best quality mattresses to ensure the best quality sleep. They study their opponents, analyzing every snap and identifying every tendency in the hope of a split-second advantage in the upcoming game. Even what little free time they have embodies an elite performer. They do brain games, which translates to a higher "football IQ," and practice meditation to improve their focus. Every aspect of their routines is meticulously crafted to enhance their performance, both in practice sessions and during games.

These athletes usually spend a pretty penny on their bodies, but wealth, status, and access to cutting-edge technology are not requirements for an elite level system. In fact, a quality system is simple and intuitive, and "upgrading to the elite package" is completely free.

START WITH SIMPLE

You've reclaimed your story and you believe it. You've conceived how it will play out successfully through visualization. With this vision, knowing the processes to get there will come intuitively.

Say you've identified as a healthy person and visualized yourself crossing the finish line of a marathon. Now, it's time to figure out how to make it a reality. As a first-timer, you need to research the best training program for your target finishing time. You can also research the very best running shoes, discover all the fancy recovery equipment promoted by your favorite athlete, upgrade your wardrobe to be 50% athleisure, and hire a trainer to help you perfect your running efficiency. Some or all of this might be helpful, but none of it will be what gets you across the finish line.

The truth is you already know what you need to do: you just need to run.

Back in Mooney Creek, I'd visualized myself succeeding in games under all types of circumstances, and that vision carried me off the gas truck and into training. Using the odometer in my car, I found that the neighbor's mailbox was a mile down the road. Every day, I ran to their mailbox and back. The daily two-mile run ensured I stayed in cardio shape. When I watched a basketball game on TV, I'd run out to the garage during commercial breaks to shoot baskets. The ceiling was only ten feet high, so my shots had no arc, and I couldn't practice layups without smashing into the wall, but reps were reps. I honed my basketball skills by dribbling the ball down the road from my home to the gas station. Occasionally, cars would pass by, and I sensed amusement from the drivers. During winter, I persuaded my uncles to let me clear a spot in their hay barn big enough to accommodate my basketball hoop, granting me additional hours for practice. My training methods were straightforward, far from glamorous or advanced. They were simple. It was my steadfast dedication to these simple routines that truly enhanced their impact.

When I recently realized my systems needed an overhaul, I began with my morning routine. A solid morning routine is at the core of effective systems. It's a common trait among the successful, but everyone has a morning routine, whether consciously designed or not. Your morning routine is where you draft your playbook for success. It's not just about what you do in your routine but align these actions with your strategic goals. Customize practices like quiet time, meditation, breath work, or affirmations to fit your objectives, just as an athlete customizes his training to his sport. In my experience, incorporating breath work into my routine was transformative. Initially approached with skepticism, it became a game-changer when I integrated it with meditation and cold plunging.

Former Pro Bowl client Nick Hardwick's work ethic underscores the power of a simple yet effective system. His relentless work ethic set him apart, embracing every task with an obsession for excellence. In his rookie season with the San Diego Chargers, his position coach suggested he draw out the plays as a study method – a strategy he embraced wholeheartedly. Night after night, for a few hours, he meticulously sketched every play from his playbook, staging each one against the eight potentially different defenses from every angle. He also dedicated himself to mastering the footwork technique of every play, repeating the steps in a rhythmic mantra: "One, two, three; one, two, three." This detailed routine ensured that by the next day, he had advanced significantly beyond those who had simply relaxed. This method wasn't just about memorization; the plays were burnt into his head. It was his commitment to exceeding expectations and maximizing his potential that was key to his 11-year NFL career.

Can you envision transforming your garage into a QB sanctuary, complete with a desk, a laptop for Zoom calls, and index cards adorned with formations, motions, run plays, passing concepts, and all kinds of snippets from the Houston Texans playbook plastered on the walls? That's precisely what my client Nick Tiano, a quarterback who honed his skills at Tennessee-Chattanooga and Mississippi State, did during the offseason leading up to training camp amidst the challenges of Covid. With the NFL Combine canceled and OTAs shifted to virtual platforms, Nick's commitment and ingenuity shone through as he immersed himself in the Texans' offensive playbook. His dedication paid off as he aced pop quizzes and tests administered by his QB coach. Facing unprecedented hurdles like those posed by Covid demands a simple yet creative mindset akin to Nick's—an elevation of standards and the creation of a personalized system geared toward maximizing success.

GET SPECIFIC

As you begin designing your systems, be as specific as possible. Duke Preston, Buccaneers, described one difference between rookies and seasoned veterans when it came to preparation. The Bucs head coach put an emphasis on spending an extra 15-30 minutes for preparation. Of course, the younger players all said, "Yeah, sure, I'll spend some extra time," but when he asked if anyone would share their process, no one spoke up. To give the young guys some pointers on how to make the most of their preparation time, Duke asked Lavonte David and Ndamukong Suh, (both perennial Pro Bowlers and Captains at the time), for their game preparation schedules, which he then shared with the younger players.

After sharing this valuable insight with the younger players, he asked them for their revised preparation schedules. Some didn't turn theirs in (which told Duke they were unwilling to be evaluated or they didn't spend the extra time). Of those who demonstrated a desire to be evaluated and quickly turned in their sheets, there was an important distinction between the rookie schedules and that of the accomplished veterans.

On the surface, the schedules looked similar. Film, recovery – the usual. The star veterans, however, were far more specific. Instead of "watch film," they wrote out the steps. "Third and long tape, short yardage, or red zone." The rookies, on the other hand, didn't include a single detail.

Specificity is important when designing your systems. Have you ever gone to the gym only to stare at the machines, clueless about what you should do or where to begin? If you've experienced this, you can attest that it probably isn't the best strategy for having a great workout. A detailed plan allows you to see all the steps, each of which has the potential to be changed or improved. It also holds you accountable for meeting or exceeding your standard.

EXECUTE A HIGHER STANDARD

You can upgrade any simple system by executing your systems at a higher standard to become an elite performer. The higher standard is the difference-maker.

In the NFL, the standard of game week preparation often predicts the result on game day. Every player practices but only the best players practice with game speed, game intensity, and game focus. Every player watches film, but the best watch film until he knows the personnel package, formation, motion, field location, and down and distance that dictates a specific play and can call out the play before the ball is snapped.

I have watched the last NFL game for many clients when neither of us knew it was going to be his last game. If he had known beforehand, he would have had his family come onto the field

> Many former players dream of playing just one more play, one more game for many years after their career is in their rear-view mirror.

and take photos with him in uniform. He would have been more intentional in his preparation, effort, and creating memories. He would have savored every step of the game day experience - putting on his uniform, doing warmups, interacting with his coaches and teammates. Many former players dream of playing just one more play, one more game for many years after their career is in their rear-view mirror. Most NFL players have a de facto "one-day contract" since they can be waived or cut anytime. Knowing that any day could be their last in the League motivates players to maintain the highest standard to avoid regrets. The truth is, any day could be our last on Earth; therefore, we, too, should maintain the highest standard we can.

One of my clients who makes a strong case as the best long-snapper in the NFL, Indianapolis Colts Luke Rhodes, earlier in his career snapped for Hall-of-Famer to-be Adam Vinatieri. I asked Luke what he sees as the differentiator for Hall-of-Fame type players.

Luke shared, "In the NFL, every player faces challenges like competition, injuries, coaching changes, and more. However, the seasoned players have navigated these hurdles with a unique mental approach to their practice, walkthroughs, treatment, and overall preparation. They go above and beyond in their routines [higher standard], both physically and mentally, which is key to their sustained success. One crucial aspect is their ability to mentally gear up for each practice session. This preparation is as vital as getting ready for the actual game because it's what ultimately leads to winning performances. These veterans understand the importance of every practice session—they know it's where games are won. They've honed the skills needed to not only secure their positions but also excel in them."

I inquired further, how do you handle high-pressure moments in the fourth quarter when every kick (and every snap) can determine the outcome of the game?

Luke shared, "We strategize about factors like wind conditions and field positions during pregame warm-ups, so we're prepared when the pressure is on. As the offense advances, my focus sharpens, visualizing the perfect snap every time. Vinnie, on the other hand, hones his mental game in solitude, mentally rehearsing his countless game-winning kicks. I just take a breath, stay calm, and execute flawlessly. For every snap that could be the game-winning kick, I trust my training and deliver a solid snap."

Before the challenges from my children, I was settling for comfort and ease in many things I did. I'd rationalize why I didn't really need to do the difficult things I'd planned on doing, and when I set goals, I gave up when it got too hard. My former consistency and discipline had been replaced by complacency. My commitment to comfort had become bigger than my commitment to growth. My systems revealed that my standard was slacking.

If you are reading this book, you're on a journey of personal growth. This commitment to personal excellence and constant improvement sets the standard for your training and lifestyle systems. If you are a player, your standard should surpass even your coach's expectations; if you have a boss, your standard should exceed your boss' standard. In fact, no one should have higher expectations for you than you do. Maybe your standard is to "leave no doubt," or maybe it is to always do what you say you're going to do. Maybe it is to do "one percent better" than you did yesterday. Maybe it is to do "whatever it takes." Maybe it is to "never give up." However you choose to think about it, your standard represents a benchmark of excellence that pushes you beyond your perceived self-imposed limitations. Let it become your compass, guiding you to outperform what others anticipate from you.

When the easier choice tempts you back into your comfort zone, remind yourself of the standard you have set. Now when

I cold plunge, if I tell myself I'm going to do three minutes, I stay in for five. When I'm climbing The Manitou Incline, (2,744 railroad tie stairs up the side of Pikes Peak Mountain) my breathlessness becomes my motivation to keep going. If I'm dreading a conversation, I silence the fear and make the call. The voice in your head telling you to stop, procrastinate, or otherwise give less than 100% effort, is the antagonist to your story. Don't let your pocket voice convince you to choose comfortable and easy. Instead, use it to motivate your inner champion.

SUMMON THE PIT CREW

Though we should never violate our standards, we are only human and sometimes fall subject to temptation, distraction, and discouragement. Furthermore, we simply don't know everything, which limits our ability to create the best processes. This is where our Pit Crew can help.

Your Pit Crew is your support team. Part of your process needs to be – I repeat: needs to be – spending quality time with people who support you.

There is no doubt that our environments influence our systems. Manipulating our environments to inspire the best systems is an effective "habit hack." However, the people in our environment are even more influential. Time spent with people who inspire, motivate, encourage, uplift, enlighten, challenge, confront, and speak truth to you is perhaps the most powerful gift you can give yourself.

My Pit Crew consists largely of my immediate family. My wife, more than anyone, has supported my dreams, challenged me to chase them, and encouraged me with both uplifting and difficult truths. My kids have inspired me with their passionate spirits as they explore new avenues of growth and adventure and have confronted me when I've fallen short of my own standards. My clients and colleagues have motivated me with their life stories of trials and triumphs and have enlightened me with nuggets of wisdom and advice.

Without a Pit Crew behind you, urging you forward, difficulty and discomfort may lead you to retreat backward in defeat. Therefore, it's imperative that you share your story with your Pit Crew. When a young man makes it to the League, his friends (if they are good friends) quickly understand that he can't party or stay out late with them, and they support this because they support his dream. In the same way, your Pit Crew should know, specifically, who you want to be, so they can hold you accountable to that dream and the systems it requires. It's easier to violate our own standards when nobody else knows what they are. On the other hand, when your partner, friend, or teammate is expecting a stellar execution of your system, slacking feels more consequential. Therefore, we're far more likely to stay true to our standard if we invite the accountability others can give us.

Your Pit Crew should also consist of people with advanced knowledge and skills. As you hone your systems, they can lend valuable insight on how to add or improve certain processes. There is no shortage of evidence that having a mentor is beneficial. Afterall, why rely on learning from your own

Teddi and me attending one of many football games.

mistakes when someone else can teach you from theirs? Consider formally asking someone to mentor or coach you. Perhaps build a system that prompts you to ask many questions whenever you're around an expert on a subject that interests you.

Surrounding yourself with trusted professionals who can help you on your way is wise. This allows you to focus on being a professional in your role. For professional athletes, their Pit Crew includes three types of professionals - body care and management, agent and financial adviser, and performance and skill trainers. A pro can only be his best when he builds and trusts his Pit Crew of professionals.

One of my clients was manipulated into taking a pay cut despite the guaranteed salary outlined in his contract. He was approached by the team president after a practice during the season. Caught off guard and not a professional negotiator, he signed the revised contract. Luckily, he called me immediately after. After a firm conversation with the team, calling them out on their schemes, the contract was placed in a drawer and never spoken of again. My client didn't have the skills or knowledge to navigate that situation with confidence, but he had someone in his corner who did.

It may seem easier to try it alone and to skip sending the Pit Crew the "New You" memo, but we aren't after easy. If you want your systems to be effective, accountable, and always improving, including your Pit Crew in your journey is essential.

UPGRADE TO ELITE

Once you've started designing your systems (starting with simple and elevating it to a higher standard), you'll begin to see how the standard can be applied to nearly every aspect of life. Systems are everywhere: the way you dress for work, the way you schedule your day, the way you prepare for a big meeting, the way you track your expenses, and the way you communicate with your clients.

After finalizing a $43 million contract in which I squeezed every last penny from the team, the jarring words from my client "Can you get me more?" hit me hard. It was a moment of realization that, while my negotiation skills were top-notch, my communication skills needed refining. I hadn't fully engaged my client in the intricate details of the negotiation's final stages. From then on, I committed to thorough communication with my clients about every step of the process, especially in the final stages, ensuring such disheartening remarks were never repeated.

Continue to expand your systems, so that every aspect of life is wrapped in intentionality. Starting with an intentional morning routine helps orient your mind for the rest of the day. That way, you carry more intention as you move through other systems throughout the day. Align each of these systems with your story, holding it to the standard your story deserves. This requires that you reflect often, actively searching for ways to improve.

> **"The way you do anything is the way you do everything."**

When you wake up, do you smile with optimism or frown with pessimism? When you eat, is it in gratitude or haste? Do you serve those around you, or focus on your own needs? Do you sit with strength, or do you slouch? Do you reach out to friends when you think of them, or put it off? Do you improve or settle? Do you spend freely or invest wisely? Do you go the extra mile or quit early? Do you do the right thing or the easy thing? As Martha Beck, a sociologist and life coach put it, "The way you do anything is the way you do everything." This is what sets the greatest apart.

Top performing NFL players are distinguished by their systems, but nothing they do is superhuman, alien, or otherwise unimaginable. Their systems are extraordinary because they hold even the most basic ones – like sleep and drinking water – to a higher standard.

If you want to be great, do everything that way. Act with integrity. Train with discipline. Seek out coaching. Show up early.

Michael Jordan set the bar exceptionally high, expecting more from himself than anyone else ever could. His benchmark was uniquely his own, a standard he alone defined. Similarly, in the NFL, the top players consistently exceed the expectations set by their coaches. They effortlessly surpass these benchmarks without any hesitation, continuously pushing beyond the standards set for them.

> Michael Jordan set the bar exceptionally high, expecting more from himself than anyone else ever could.

If you want to almost be great, do only what is asked or required. Show up just in time...

I met with the Arizona Cardinals to discuss a contract extension for a starting player I represented. The general manager invited Head Coach Ken Whisenhunt into our meeting, who shared, "I don't want to give a big contract to a 7:29er." He went on to explain that a 7:29er is a player who arrives just in time for the daily 7:30 a.m. meetings, contingent upon a perfect drive to work by hitting all green lights. Coach Whisenhunt was clear that my client needed to demonstrate maturity and better punctuality before the organization would consider a significant contract. Despite my client's talent, his failure to have a higher standard for punctuality limited his NFL potential. Having a high standard on a holistic level is critical.

In sports there are many players who have experienced perceived unfairness, lack of reps or playing time, and want to blame their coaches. Instead, I tell my clients and my boys that the key to these challenges is to have such a high standard of performance their coaches would be stupid not to play them. Make it undebatable and indisputable!

From his hometown in Anchorage, Alaska, through college at North Dakota playing Division II, and then becoming a 5th round Draft pick for the Denver Broncos, Chris Kuper not only solidified his role as an offensive guard in the Broncos' starting lineup but also reached a Pro Bowl level before a significant lower leg injury. In his rookie year, Chris absorbed the essence of a "pro standard" from seasoned veteran center, Tom Nalen, a perennial Pro Bowler in his mid-thirties. It is a big jump for college football players transitioning from Division II to the NFL. Those who manage this leap often have exceptional role models and the wisdom to emulate the best practices, which Chris personified. Presently, as the offensive line coach for the Minnesota Vikings, Chris embodies an open-minded coaching approach, valuing standards over beginnings, a testament to his own journey and growth.

In the NFL, players aren't told they need to come in early, or how long they need to spend watching film, or what they need to eat. The standard is theirs to set. Thus, how high they set their standard and how holistically they apply it determines their performance level. It's the same in life. You don't need to wake up thirty minutes early, or call your mom, or try a cold shower, or take the first step, or skip junk food, or buy your wife flowers, or spellcheck your emails. You get to design your systems, and you get to set your standard. Your systems should reflect the reverence you have for your story. Do yours?

"Raise your standards and the universe will meet you there." - **Tony Robbins**

CHAPTER 5 RECAP

Your systems consist of your habits, routines, and focused training.

Our Standard is built by and backed by our systems: we must allow our belief to drive our actions, and our actions to reinforce our belief.

- Start with Simple: Your systems don't need to be overly complex. Morning routines are a perfect place to start.

- Get Specific: Creating a detailed plan improves accountability.

- Execute a Higher Standard: Execute your system with a commitment to personal excellence and constant improvement.

- Summon the Pit Crew: Inform your loved ones and peers of your story, system, and standard. Their support and accountability are essential. Gain wisdom from knowledgeable mentors.

- Upgrade to Elite: Apply your standard to every system.

Standards to Live by:
- Never Give Up

- Leave No Doubt

- Whatever It Takes

- Give it Everything You Got

- One Percent Better

Pro Tip

The way you do anything
is the way you do everything.

6

Plug into Your Purpose

P URPOSE IS THE UNDERLYING intention or reason that drives an individual, offering a sense of meaning, direction, and fulfillment in their actions and life choices. Many are uncertain how to discover their purpose. Every NFL player, upon concluding their football career, faces the task of finding a new sense of purpose beyond football.

I advocate a three-step approach to uncovering your purpose: (1) Identify what you enjoy doing irrespective of monetary or status considerations, (2) Recognize your talents or abilities that come naturally to you, and (3) Lean into what God calls you to do. The convergence of these three elements will illuminate your true purpose.

Finding your purpose often involves challenges. Your purpose does not mean easy. Doing hard things isn't easy. That may sound like common sense, but so often, people desire greatness without submitting to the difficult processes that greatness requires.

My son Brock shared his perspective on hard: "What I love about football is how much football asks of you, especially as a QB. Your entire life needs to be dedicated to it. I just love how you must be all in. And I love it because I'm willing to be all in. I love knowing that I have that edge on a lot of people because I'm willing to go through more."

Brock continued, "I give you the credit for sharing all the stories of your players getting cut or facing a lot of adversity. When adversity hit me in college, it wasn't a surprise. It didn't make it any less hard, I just knew this was the path from the jump. We (he and his brother) knew damn well what came with this football journey. We both knew it was going to be a lot of adversity; we never thought it was going to be easy. We knew what we signed up for. Football breaks your heart every single year, but we still go back to it because we love it that much. Honestly, you don't know what you're made of until you're at rock bottom and you've got to climb back up. And man, that's an addicting feeling when you're at rock bottom and you still have the confidence that you can still achieve everything you want to achieve because you have that belief in yourself. No one can take that from you, and that's addicting as hell!" This response shows Brock was plugged into his purpose despite the adversity and circumstances he faced.

Envision high school football as a form of Special Forces Boot Camp, a challenging endeavor not meant for the faint-hearted. These young athletes commit over two hours each day after school, opting for the rigor of shoulder pads and the grit of the field over the comfort of video games and relaxation. They engage in physical battles, going head-to-head with peers who might be stronger or quicker, enduring the elements, from frozen hands in snowstorms to the relentless sun and heat.

But what drives them through this demanding regimen, beyond the bruises, the risks of injury, and the extreme weather conditions? It's the sense of camaraderie and belonging to something greater than themselves. For some, it's the energy from the cheering crowd, their peers whose expectations they strive to meet, fueling them with a deep sense of school spirit. For some, it's the town's pride and the painted windows of local businesses and the old men in the local diner encouraging them to beat the rival, or to make it to state.

For many, it's more personal - the smile of a certain special someone in the stands or the proud gaze of a grandparent watching from afar. Some play with the hope of securing a college scholarship, dreaming of making their family proud. But perhaps the most compelling is the bond they share with their teammates - their "brothers in arms" in the football realm. In the huddle, they find unity and purpose, a collective drive that propels them to push past their limits, withstand the trials, and chase the glory of victory together. In each of these cases, they feel part of something larger than themselves, and this pushes them through the workouts, through the weather, and toward the win.

When things get difficult – and remember, we aren't after easy here – plugging back into your purpose is key.

> 66
> Purpose is the deeper mission that fuels your commitment to being your best self.
> 99

If you still aren't clear on your purpose, enduring discomfort will be difficult. Remember, purpose is the deeper mission that fuels your commitment to being your best self. It's the beacon of Pro Mindset that aligns your actions with your values, leads you to set courageous goals, and motivates you to serve something larger.

Reflect on the passage from John 21:6, where Jesus, standing on the shore of the Sea of Galilee, calls out to his disciples, "Friends, haven't you any fish?" From their boat, the disciples respond with a simple "no." To this, Jesus advises, "Throw your net on the right side of the boat, and you will find some." Acting on Jesus' instruction, despite it being just a shift of 7.5 feet from their original spot, the disciples cast their net. Astonishingly, they caught so many fish they couldn't draw the net back in. Consider your own path: What is your purpose? Where is your "7.5 feet"—that small shift that could lead to greater direction, resilience, and fulfillment?

DIRECTION

Clear purpose furnishes us with a blueprint for success. With clarity of purpose, we are unafraid to set audacious goals. Imagine an NFL player who is crystal clear on his purpose: to glorify God by using His gifts to the best of his ability, provide for his family, and be the best husband he can be. With a clear focus on a divine purpose, he's unintimidated to claim the bold goal of becoming a Hall-of-Famer. He understands that God put him in a specific circumstance, with specific talents and blessings, at a specific time, to use him in an extraordinary way. He also understands that to realize his full potential, he must give himself wholly to the process, in his effort, and in his belief.

This purpose harmonizes his goals with his actions even when the stakes are seemingly low. Let's say this player's wife prefers that he fold his towel neatly, but she doesn't care enough to complain if it's sloppily thrown over the towel bar instead. The action itself – taking the extra time to fold his towel – has a very low connection to an outcome and, therefore, seems inconsequential. However, his purpose of being the best husband he can be sustains his commitment to honor his wife in even the smallest of details, and these small details accumulate.

Purpose also aligns our goals and actions when the goals are long-term. When actions are linked to a distant outcome, committing to your systems seems less urgent, and it's tempting to procrastinate. Staying disciplined is easy when the pressure is on, but how do you manage your systems when time is not of the essence, and you have total freedom?

It is normal to question your purpose when the dream seems far in the distance. When my son JoJo was in college, playing linebacker at Nebraska, he reached out to me at a time when many of his peers not involved in football were graduating and starting their careers. Our conversation unfolded like this:

JoJo inquired, "Hey, what should I do next?" I responded, slightly puzzled, "What do you mean by 'what should you do?'" He elaborated, "I mean, what should I do if football doesn't pan out?"

At that moment, unsure if he would even get a chance in the NFL, I advised, "If you're serious about making football part of your future, you need to put aside thoughts of a Plan B right now." I further explained, "Focusing on a Plan B might lead you to settle for it as your Plan A."

The conversation concluded there, JoJo stayed focused on his football dream, and today he is playing in the NFL.

One challenge for NFL players is taking true time-off during the off-season. Consider our hypothetical player with the goal of being a Hall-of-Famer. Counterintuitively, having a clear purpose regarding football helps him spend intentional time away from it. Afterall, if his purpose is to glorify God by using His gifts to the best of his ability, provide for his family, and to be the best husband he can be, the off-season must in part be utilized to relax and get his life in balance. Desperation and anxiety have no room to invade this sacred decompression time with friends and family. Because he is confident in his purpose, he holds this important system of rest to a higher standard.

Then, when the allotted time for mental vacation is over, it's an entirely different challenge to return to rigorous training. A few months can misleadingly seem like plenty of time, tempting players to slack off or procrastinate. He could rationalize, "I don't really need to do my cardio plan for today," and he might be right to an extent. He'll probably be in fine-enough shape by the time OTA practices come around. But because he is laser-focused on his purpose, he's ready to double down on training, excited to come back healthier, stronger, faster, and more mentally prepared than ever.

Though a long-term goal might seem too far in the future for today's systems to matter, the off-season is what prepares you for game day. Purpose-driven players infuse it into everything they do. When they're on vacation, they do that exceptionally. When they're training, they do that exceptionally too. When they train intentionally day after day - they "stack 'em." When you are clear on your purpose for everything, it becomes much easier to give it your full focus and effort, consistently, day-after-day.

When there is no good purpose for our actions, it signals that it's time to make a change. I'll never forget attending one of my daughter Rylee's soccer games when she was about ten years old and playing goalkeeper. I spent most of the game on the phone with clients and teams. When I looked over at Rylee to see how the game was going, she was almost as focused on the game as I was! Her body language (dancing and twirling around) indicated that her mind was elsewhere. On the way home, I asked her if she liked soccer, to which she replied, "Oh, no, Daddy!" I asked her why she played soccer, and she replied, obediently and emphatically, "Because you and Mommy take me to practice and games!"

Children ask, "Why?" all the time. They're oriented towards discovering purpose, and a desire to match actions to reason. Rylee was clear about why she played soccer. As reasonable parents, we knew that "just to please her parents" was not an acceptable reason. That was Rylee's final soccer season. My wife Teddi and I paid closer attention to what activities she enjoyed and did during her spare time, and our soccer carpool routes evolved into theater, voice lessons, and dance competitions!

For many people, this conversation doesn't happen early on. The child stays in soccer. The man stays at the job he hates. The bad habit stays around. They don't ask themselves, "Why am I doing this?" and eventually confuse or forget the real purpose. The child convinces herself "she likes soccer" when she just wants to make her parents proud. The man stays in the job "for his family," but he's miserable, which spills into his attitude and the way he treats his wife and kids. The habit is to "let off steam," but truthfully, the addiction is the source of your stress. It helps us check in with ourselves about the purpose of our systems. Why am I doing this? If your purpose is faulty or unclear, your systems will be misguided.

Purpose gives us direction, guiding the creation of and revisions of our systems. It aligns our actions with our goals, which keeps us moving forward when our actions seem insignificant, reminding us why each system deserves the best version of ourselves, today.

> " Purpose gives us direction, guiding the creation of and revisions of our systems. "

OVERCOME ADVERSITY

Challenges and setbacks invite identity killers to steal our confidence and knock us off our path. Purpose equips us to persevere through hardship.

When we are committed to our systems but aren't seeing results, burnout threatens to kill our motivation. My son Brock has played quarterback throughout high school, college and now in Germany. Because only one quarterback plays on a team, his journey has been marked by constant competition and adversity. QB2s (backup quarterbacks) must consistently strive to prove their value, preparing like a starter, but knowing they'll likely receive no playing time. How do you respond when your highest-standard systems show little to no results? Putting in 100% effort and self-belief can be exhausting when you're still second-string.

Throughout it all, Brock has displayed an unwavering commitment to his purpose, even when his circumstances didn't align with his story.

In high school, Brock was his big brother's quarterback, which was difficult at times. If he didn't throw to his brother, JoJo would chew him out in the huddle, undermining his leadership on the team. Though this brother-teammate dynamic was difficult to manage, it prepared Brock to deal with egotistical receivers who believe they are entitled to the ball on every pass play, and it taught him that "people cannot take your power away from you, but you can give them your power."

Brock (#15), me and JoJo (#12) after a high school game.

Brock's success in high school, including three state titles, didn't immediately earn him college recognition. At Ventura Community College, he took his team to the Southern California Championship and won to demonstrate his ability under pressure. Brock accepted a full-ride scholarship at Campbell University, where, despite his confidence and preparedness, Brock redshirted.

Brock made the decision to return to junior college. Transferring to Independence Community College, famously known as Last Chance U, felt like a step backward. However, Brock's definition of perseverance is, "seeing things through," and knowing that "things get the toughest right before the breakthrough." At Last Chance U, he showed up to find seven quarterbacks when he'd been told there would only be three quarterback competitors. Feeling betrayed and deceived, he could have abandoned his sense of purpose on the team and lowered his standards. Instead, he doubled down on his purpose, using it to his advantage. Since all the other quarterbacks had been told the same thing, he controlled his reaction and focused on his own performance instead of the coach's misrepresentations. His response earned Brock the QB1 spot and All-American status, led his team to a winning record, and earned him a D1 scholarship.

When Brock's D1 Power 5 dream came true and he accepted a scholarship to the University of Louisville, the challenges were not over. Brock describes his journey in terms of "hitting new levels." Each new level of accomplishment boosted his confidence in some ways while simultaneously unearthing a deeper level of insecurity in others.

Brock started four games and went 3-1 including a Fenway Bowl game victory at the end of the 2022 season. Then Louisville had a coaching change heading into his final season. The new coaches brought in another quarterback to fill the QB1 spot, putting Brock in the position to compete for QB2 with seven other QBs, and the identity killer of comparison became stronger than ever. But once again, Brock didn't allow the setback to discourage him. Amidst the uncertainty, he learned to surrender his expectations of the outcome and instead focused on his process. Because people are naturally incentive-based, unwilling to put in the effort if there is no reward, he changed his mindset to detach from football outcomes and think instead about who he was becoming as a man. This clear sense of purpose led him to "seize all the mundane days when it seemed like nothing was going to happen. That's how legends are created. They're legends in the dark and then one day, the spotlight comes to them."

Brock, #19, leading his Louisville Cardinals to a 2022 Fenway Bowl victory!

By addressing and overcoming this new level of challenge, Brock unlocked an even deeper level of self-belief and belief in his Creator. "When God has placed something in my life and anoints me, it'll come to pass."

> **When God has placed something in my life and anoints me, it'll come to pass.**

Plugging into your purpose gives you the resiliency to endure the challenges that will inevitably keep coming. When you reach the next level of success, you can expect a new level of hard, but each challenge is an opportunity to grow to new heights and deeper belief. "I'm starting to realize when you are truly living out your dreams, that's going to be the case," Brock concludes. "Every year I say the same thing: it was the hardest season of my life, and it was the most rewarding season in my life."

JoJo grew through setbacks in college as well. During his six years at the University of Nebraska, JoJo tore his ACL. His teammates and coaches supported him as he worked hard at physical therapy, eager to return to the game, but after seeing his hard work and patience pay off, he tore his ACL in the same knee again seven months later. The second time, no one came to see him in the hospital except for his mother, girlfriend, and me. Teammates and coaches were dismissive of him in the stadium. The sentiment in the air was clear: they believed JoJo was no longer valuable to the team. As his father, I told him, "If you ever wanted to quit football, now would be the time. Nobody would blame or question you." Just getting down the 12 stairs to his bedroom became a grueling, tedious challenge that questioned his purpose for playing football and reminded him of the choice in front of him. Did he really want to keep putting his body through this? Was the sport really worth it to him?

Setbacks are more than a blow to our pride or a hindrance to our plan. They can be physically painful, affecting every aspect of our daily life, and just when you think you've overcome it, they can knock you back down even harder. You can abandon your purpose because of the pain and challenge, or you can use the painful, challenging moments you didn't plan to question, resolve, and meditate on your purpose. If you choose the latter, you will be even more resilient to future setbacks. Despite his successful rookie season with the Indianapolis Colts, JoJo was released at the end of his second training camp with an injury. I watched proudly as my son handled the uncertainty with a confident, calm resolve. He rehabbed, waited, and trained patiently for his name to be called, and when it was (by the Tennessee Titans), he was ready. He played the final five games of the 2023 season.

Ryan Lilja encountered adversity just before his senior year of high school, preventing him from playing football that season. Despite being a zero-star prospect, he went the Kansas junior college route before Kansas State's Head Coach Bill Snyder recognized his potential and offered him a scholarship at Kansas State during their prime years in the early 2000s. Enduring repetitive ankle injuries during his college senior year, Ryan needed painkiller injections to play on Saturdays, showcasing mental toughness, high football IQ and the ability to overcome obstacles.

I remember a moment outside Arrowhead Stadium after the Big 12 Championship Game, where Ryan shared he struggled with "feeling" his ankles. I had never had a prospect share that with me. Uncertain about signing him, my coaching friend Bret Bielema praised Ryan's mental toughness, ultimately influencing my decision to sign Ryan. After signing with me, a medical evaluation uncovered dead tissue in Ryan's ankles, necessitating months of rest. Meanwhile, his peers were training for the

NFL's Pre-Draft Evaluation events, such as the All-Star games and the Combine. Unfortunately, Ryan missed these crucial opportunities. When NFL scouts attended his Pro Day in March, Ryan had limited physical preparation, resulting in a less-than-ideal performance. As expected, he went undrafted, his name not called during the Draft weekend.

However, Coach Snyder's endorsement to then Kansas City Chiefs Head Coach Dick Vermeil changed Ryan's trajectory as his hometown Chiefs signed Ryan to an undrafted free agent contract. Ryan went on to start more than 100 NFL games and played a pivotal role as a starting offensive guard on the Indianapolis Colts Super Bowl XLI winning team. His journey is a testament to his unwavering perseverance in the face of adversity. Ryan did not allow his lack of opportunity out of high school or college to limit his success in the NFL. Ryan was deeply connected to his purpose in football and did not let his tough circumstances detract him.

FULFILLMENT

Purpose satisfies us in a way that transcends self-centeredness. People with clear purpose inspire, motivate, and uplift others.

My daughter Rylee is an oracle who's helped hundreds of clients find their "deeper why" since opening her practice. Oftentimes, she helps clients uncover a dream they've never been confident enough to voice. When I asked Rylee how people can balance the internal and external stimuli contributing to their sense of purpose, she described the "eternal essence" or soul, which is the "unchanging, deeper part of who we are," and the ego, which consists of our preferences and personality. Though our ego plays an extremely important role ("It's what makes [you] magnetic. It's that zing."), it can get out of balance. Oftentimes, one or more "dials" – whether it be ego, fear, or programming – become too loud and drown out the "soul's voice." When this happens, we feel disconnected from our purpose. "Learning to harness the power of your ego to be in service to the soul" allows us not only to make a deep impact, but to experience a profound level of fulfillment and satisfaction.

I had Laura Okmin, NFL Hall-of-Fame Reporter as a guest on Pro Mindset Podcast. When Laura set her sights on sports broadcasting, everyone told her she couldn't and shouldn't do it. Her family would ask about her Plan B, but as she puts it, her Plan B was to get her Plan A to work. She knew she had a knack for getting people to open up, and though her talent wasn't there yet, she was committed to her dream. "I knew that I would be good at it," she remembers.

Laura's dream came true, but when she stepped into the world of sports broadcasting, she found herself in a man's game, a landscape that questioned her very presence. Like many athletes who make it to the professional level, she found that living the dream was riddled with difficulty. The doubts were no longer external; they became her internal narrative. Her self-doubt manifested in feeling the need to constantly prove herself. For example, she would explain basic football concepts like the difference between a 3-4 front a 4-3 front in her questions to gain credibility.

Losing her mother to cancer had left a hole in her heart, and desiring to make her mother proud, Laura poured herself into her work. As she became the voice of the game, her own voice started to fade. She hid behind stories, concealing her emotions, her sadness, and her depression. Not wanting to seem ungrateful in her dream job, she built up a happy façade.

Laura on the sidelines of an NFL game.

Many pro athletes deal with this same issue. They've confused their deep purpose with their desired outcome, and when they achieve their desired outcome of making it to the League, they wonder why they feel so unfulfilled. They pretend gratitude while underneath they feel lost.

It took many years and a dance with death for Laura to see through her own illusion. Everyone thought the plane was going down, and as passengers around her cried and scrambled to make phone calls, she just sat, realizing she didn't care. When the plane finally landed, she vowed to live a life she'd care about not losing.

Laura reflected on her purpose and realized that her drive to make her mother proud was misguided. How could she honor someone's life by not living her own? She began to turn down the ego-driven dials of doubt, people-pleasing, and achievement, and tuned back into her soul. Sure, she'd done some amazing things throughout her career, but what mattered was not what she'd done, but who she was. With the dials in balance, she was able to be her authentic self and even empower others to do the same. She started her organization, GALvanize, to give women in the sports world a network of support. She trains them to be on camera, but her first and foremost focus is building their confidence off-camera. In addition to all the stories she'd enjoyed telling over the years, the "highlight tape" of her career now features ventures that are meaningful to her, including multiple scholarship establishments, a children's book for kids whose parent has cancer, and a production company with purposeful messaging.

> **❝** When you merge your conscious headspace (your story) with your purposeful processes (your standards) you manifest your peak performance (your stage). **❞**

Laura's transformation moved her beyond the external validation and the superficial aspects of her profession. Her journey reflects the challenges and triumphs of being a woman in a male-dominated world, but more importantly, it underscores the universal struggle to align our professional and personal selves. Laura's Pro Mindset is a reminder that the real victory is not just in achieving professional success, but in finding personal fulfillment, empathy, and authenticity in what we do. When we are "living the dream" through the eyes of others, we lose ourselves. But when we become the main actors in our own dreams by living our purpose, we find both personal fulfillment and the ability to selflessly serve those around us.

The effectiveness of your systems hinges on their connection to your purpose. Do your systems align with your purpose? Are they driven by a clear goal, designed to help you reach your dreams?

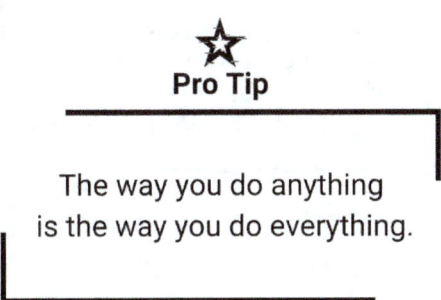

★
Pro Tip

The way you do anything
is the way you do everything.

The typical NFL journey often ends abruptly due to the unavoidable roster squeeze. In training camp 90 players vie for spots, yet only 53 secure positions on the active roster. Unlike the rare longevity seen in someone like Tom Brady, who played for 23 seasons, most players lack control over their careers. Roughly 95% of players don't experience the fanfare of a post-retirement celebration, often exiting without much fanfare.

One of my clients, Mike Lehan, a fifth-round defensive back from the University of Minnesota, chose to depart before the league could push him out. After six NFL seasons marked by injuries, he felt he had fulfilled his football purpose and was ready to embrace life beyond the NFL. Despite tempting offers, including a lucrative contract from the New Orleans Saints with a seven-figure signing bonus, Mike stayed true to his decision. Even a persuasive email from the Saints' GM couldn't sway him. He recognized that his identity extended far beyond being an NFL player. Transitioning seamlessly into the real world, he never looked back and now serves as the Senior VP and Head of School at the IMG Academy in Bradenton, FL. Mike's journey highlights the importance of recognizing when one has outgrown a dream and finding a new, fulfilling purpose.

Pro Tip

Purposeful practice is the cornerstone of growth because true success doesn't happen by accident. True success happens on purpose.

CHAPTER 6 RECAP

The 3-step approach to uncovering your purpose:

(1) **Identify** what you enjoy doing irrespective of monetary or status considerations,

(2) **Recognize** your natural talents and gifted abilities, and

(3) **Lean** into what God calls you to do.

Purpose gives our systems direction, resilience, and fulfillment.

Direction:

- Purpose leads us to set audacious goals.

- Purpose aligns our actions with our goals even when the actions seem insignificant.

- Purpose motivates us when our actions seem non-urgent.

- A lack of good purpose signals the need for change.

Overcome Adversity (Resilience):

- Identity killers will try to knock us off our path when setbacks arise; purpose helps us endure.

- Purpose encourages us when we don't see the desired outcomes.

Fulfillment:

- When ego, fear, or programming are too loud, we tend to disconnect from our deeper purpose.

- Purpose helps us use the power of our ego in service to the soul.

- Purpose allows us to act authentically as the main character in our dreams rather than through the eyes of others.

- Purpose leads us to selflessly serve others.

- You will know when you have outgrown your current purpose.

Pro Tip

Purposeful practice is the cornerstone of growth because true success doesn't happen by accident. True success happens on purpose.

7

Show up

YOU LACE UP YOUR cleats and stand up before the knot in your stomach can make its way to your throat. You jump up and down. You shake your arms. The energy is in you and all around you. Someone hits you on your shoulder pads. Beyond the sea of shoulder pads, you see a rectangle of light. Your feet move you towards it, and as it grows, so does the noise. The low rumble is becoming louder and clearer. Arms are waving down at you from above, and then – your feet hit the familiar feel of the field.

Welcome to your stage!

The curtain has opened. The lights have come up. Dress rehearsal is over, and the audience has taken their seats. It's showtime.

You know that point in the movie. It's their shot at their dream job, it's the big game, it's the epic battle between the hero and the villain, it's the man on one knee! It's their chance! It's the moment we've all been waiting for! It's their stage.

Will you win your stage? That depends. First, you need to define what your stage is.

Your stage is your time to shine; it's what you've been preparing for. It could be on a field or a court, in a theater, or in an office. It could be at a podium or a pulpit. It could be an interview, pitch, speech, or presentation. It could be the phone call of forgiveness after years of not speaking. It could be moving in with your new spouse or bringing your baby home from the hospital for the first time. It could be taking off the training wheels or getting out of rehab. Consider what big moments you're preparing for. What opportunities to shine are awaiting you?

Now, with this climatic moment in your mind, ask yourself: am I going to show up for it? Am I going to show all the way up for it?

When my son JoJo was a sophomore in high school, he was recognized as a talented player expected to make significant contributions, with the coaches eyeing him for the starting safety position. However, during Fall camp, a senior teammate repeatedly sent JoJo off the field whenever the defensive coordinator put him in. Respecting his teammate, JoJo stepped aside, forfeiting his practice reps. As a result, the coaches didn't start him in the first game of the season.

From being on the coaching staff, I knew they wanted JoJo to start, but they felt he needed to demonstrate more confidence and stand up to his senior teammate.

On the morning of his first game, I prepared a pregame breakfast for JoJo. It was then that he opened up, asking me why he wasn't starting despite feeling he deserved the spot. "I'm glad you asked," I replied and went on to explain that the coaches were waiting for him to assert himself – to act like a man and claim his position rather than wait for his senior teammate's approval. In the next game, when the senior, exhausted from his offensive duties, allowed a touchdown pass, the defensive coordinator put JoJo in the game. JoJo seized the opportunity. He finally "showed up" for his stage, and he secured his spot for the rest of his high school career.

JoJo's first start marked the beginning of a great run for Pine Creek H.S., and the program achieved an impressive record of 37-2 during JoJo's tenure as a starter. When you think you're ready to play, but you can't stand up to a teammate, perhaps you are not ready to perform in the arena. Coaches will very rarely believe in a player more than he believes in himself. The coaches were not going to believe in JoJo until he owned his worth and showed up embodying it.

Fully showing up for life's biggest moments involves embracing your identity, new story, and bringing all the confidence you've gained from your thorough preparation. 100% belief in yourself and robust confidence are required or else you'll crumble under the weight of all eyes on you.

CUT LOOSE THE TRAINING PARACHUTE

Athletes often incorporate a training parachute into their speed improvement routines, using it to add resistance and hone their focus on body lean and power. The underlying concept, both in training and psychologically, is that in post-parachute sprinting (the race), the athlete will experience a sense of lightness, increased speed, and improved overall velocity. However, a common challenge faced by many athletes is the tendency to carry mental baggage like a training parachute into actual competitions, hindering their performance with unproductive thoughts. This phenomenon is particularly evident when athletes participate in events like the NFL Combine's 40-yard sprint, where they strive to feel light, move swiftly, and avoid any mental or physical obstacles that might impede their progress.

In the NFL, there are many stages, i.e., the stage is the starting line in Lucas Oil Stadium getting ready to run your Combine 40, NFL Draft Weekend when your phone rings, the first time you show up at your team's headquarters for Rookie Minicamp, reporting for NFL Training Camp, or running out of the tunnel for your first NFL game. NFL Training Camp presents an intensely stressful and competitive environment, particularly for rookies. It stands out as the "biggest" stage a rookie is likely to face early in his career. A player's friends and family are intimately aware that he is competing for a roster spot, and everyone knows how things are going. They only need to look at social media or a quick Google search to check up on practice reports during training camp to see daily performance reviews. Whether he dropped a ball, had a great play, missed a tackle, fumbled, had an interception, or made a mistake, everyone knows. Everyone who is interested watches in real time to see whether the player has what it takes to be an NFL player.

A young man's rookie year in the NFL is one of the most difficult tests he will ever face. He needs a strong identity code. One of my former clients had an NFL-ready identity. David Diehl was a fifth-round pick of the New York Giants in 2005. "Hollywood" was David's college nickname. After he was drafted by the Giants, Hollywood flew to New York for the offseason program. I spoke with David during OTAs and was interested in how he was acclimating to the Giants organization and locker room. I can usually detect how a player is doing – how much confidence and belief he has in himself – by whether he is connecting with his coaches, veteran teammates, or just the other rookies.

I asked him about his weekend activities. He said he went to a barbecue at Tiki Barber's home, the Giants star running back. I asked him who else was there. He mentioned Eli Manning, Michael Strahan, and Jeremy Shockey – the established stars for the Giants at the time. When David shared the names of his teammates, I assumed that everyone had been invited, but he said he was the only rookie there. My probing continued. I knew David didn't have a car, so I inquired about how he got there (this was before Uber), and he shared that Strahan lent him one of his extra cars because he could only drive one at a time! Strahan told David to return the car once he was able to buy his own.

That conversation showed me everything I needed to know about David's mental state. A rookie must believe in himself to hang out with the team's stars. As a result, it came as no surprise when the season began, and David was named the Giants' opening day starter on the offensive line as a rookie.

David holding the Lombardi trophy after a Giants Super Bowl win.

David's identity (intelligent, confident, and toughness) was aligned with his dreams rather than with his circumstances as a fifth rounder. Most fifth-round picks do not start the opening game of their rookie season. Many fifth-round picks do not even make the 53-man roster. More impressively, most fifth-round picks do not have 11-year careers.

David played every position on the offensive line except center and started the first 120 regular season games of his career. By the time he hung up his cleats, he had started 160 of 164 regular season games and 11 postseason outings, including victories in Super Bowls XLII and XLVI.

David's identity as a rookie was consistent with the identity of an NFL starter. David did not show up in New York with the mindset of making the practice squad or hoping to make the 53-man roster like a lot of 5th rounders. Instead, David "Hollywood" Diehl showed up embodying his story and his worth. He "was who he was" and others saw it, too – he was a Pro Bowler.

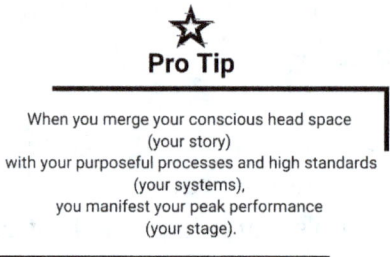

Pro Tip

When you merge your conscious head space
(your story)
with your purposeful processes and high standards
(your systems),
you manifest your peak performance
(your stage).

Writing a New Story + Standardizing your Systems = Winning your Stage!

As we discussed earlier, your stage is your time to shine, and the moment you've been preparing for. But it's not always the climatic, crowd-chanting, curtain-opening moment you might have imagined. It's not just the championship games but also the way you carry yourself in meetings. It's not just the big presentation but also your daily professionalism and attention to detail. It's not just the day you bring the baby home from the hospital, but also every sleepless night and messy room and teenager-fueled argument thereafter. It's not just the speech from the podium but also the brief interaction in the elevator.

When you really think about it, any moment can be your time to shine, and if you show up for it, big opportunities and crucial moments will unfold. It's all your stage.

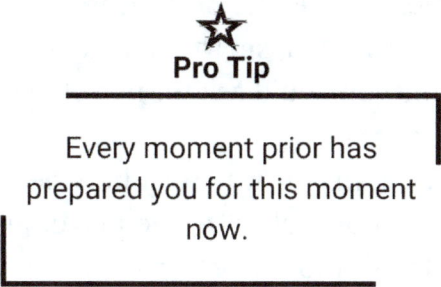

Pro Tip

Every moment prior has prepared you for this moment now.

Years ago, I was recruiting an offensive lineman from Oklahoma, Chris Chester, who I knew would be drafted in the early rounds. About a week before his Bowl game, he called to tell me he was going to sign with CAA, the biggest agency in the business at that time. It was disappointing news. I was also recruiting one of his teammates, so I went to the Holiday Bowl, where I ran into the young man's father. I wished them the best and made cordial small talk. When I said, "I bet Chris is excited that CAA is here to see him," his father looked a bit puzzled and corrected me. "No, no, CAA is not coming."

Now I was puzzled. "Well, I saw CAA in the team hotel lobby. Are you sure they're not scheduled to meet?" They were likely recruiting multiple players in the Bowl game, but surely, they'd make a point to see Chris if they came out for the game.

After the game, I received a text. CAA hadn't said hello to Chris at all. Chris' dad invited me to a meeting the next morning in San Diego, and the first thing out of Chris' mouth was, "You still want me?"

The CAA agent hadn't realized the gravity of his stage at that Bowl game. He showed up for one player but failed to show up for another. I didn't know at the time that my stage was this small talk with a former recruit's father, but the interaction led Chris to signing with me. He was the 56th overall pick and played for 11 years. Chris was talented, smart, dedicated, had a great family and he's everything you could ask for in a client.

In another story, a player was torn between me and another agent. Still unsure who to choose, the player and his fiancé met the other agent for dinner. The dinner went well, but right as they were leaving, the agent made a point to insult me personally. He knew I was competing against him for the recruit, and he let comparison and desperation get the better of him, thinking the insult would sway the player in his favor. As soon as the player and his fiancé got to the car, they looked at each other knowingly. This agent's lack of confidence was a huge red flag, and though they had been torn before, their decision now was clear. In an attempt to destroy his competition, his insult actually worked against him.

Every moment has the potential to be a stage, and depending on what version of you shows up, you'll either be delighted or dismayed by the pivotal moments.

A few years into his career, Brock Gutierrez, a backup offensive center client with the Cincinnati Bengals, encountered a formidable challenge during Training Camp. He was up against a rookie third-round Draft pick. Brock's position coach, Paul Alexander, candidly told Brock that the rookie was earmarked as the future starter, but Brock remained undeterred. Even when his practice reps were reduced to third-team status, he kept his focus. He continued to show up with a starter mentality, refusing to adopt a mindset of defeat.

In a critical final preseason game against the Colts, Coach Al gave Brock a simple directive, "Go make it happen!" Unexpectedly, Brock played the right guard, center, and left guard positions each for a full quarter. Brock hadn't practiced or taken reps at either guard position during Training Camp. This stage was not what he expected, and doubt could've easily taken over. He could've said, "I'm not that guy." If he'd focused on the practice and reps he was lacking, his performance probably would have reflected his inexperience. Instead, he said, "I am that guy," and showed up as a clutch, confident player. Displaying remarkable adaptability and resilience, Brock excelled in these unfamiliar roles. Despite his position coach's early skepticism, Brock's ability to show up on the unexpected stage secured his job on the active 53-man roster.

Someone who knows how to win a stage is my wife, Teddi. Teddi grew up competing in 4-H, then pageants, won Miss Rodeo Kansas, competed in Miss Rodeo America, and later built a successful career in sports marketing, working for McDonald's Corporation on the Olympics, World Cup, NFL, NHRA, and McDonald's All-American High School Basketball Game, and the United States Olympic Committee. Her thorough preparation allowed her to stand confidently in her self-worth whether the stage was a pageant or the male-dominated sports field. Knowing that parts of a stage are uncontrollable, she focused on what she could control. She prepared even more when her credibility was in question, stood tall, exuded positive energy, and she always smiled. "When you just share a smile, it opens a lot of people's hearts," she advises.

Teddi became the queen before she was crowned. She researched the expectations of the role and stepped into it before she ever won. "I wasn't just a mere competitor passively saying,

'Choose me, choose me,'" she recalls. "No, I was being the queen." Later, when she was a judge evaluating queen candidates, her discernment came from observing their demeanor. "Their body language, the way they spoke, and their overall energy revealed a lot. It was evident in the way they conducted themselves whether they already embodied the essence of a queen or not. Thus, it was quite straightforward for me to... simply scan the room and recognize who already possessed the grace and confidence of wearing the crown."

Showing up to any stage with confidence is the key to winning crucial moments. Studies show that striking a "superhero" before a big presentation boosts confidence, which positively impacts performance. You don't necessarily need to imitate Superman before every opportunity, especially because we don't always know when these opportunities will arise. However, when you acknowledge and define your stage – no matter how unexpected, small, or insignificant – remind yourself just WHO is showing up for it (your Pro self). If you embody that person entirely and reject any imposter syndrome or insecurity that may arise, you can manifest your peak performance and win the stage.

CHAPTER 7 RECAP

Your stage is:

- Your time to shine

- What you've been preparing for

- Any pivotal space where big opportunities and crucial moments unfold

Define your stage, even when it is unexpected or seemingly insignificant.

Decide "who" is going to show up for it. (Your best, most confident self)

Reject insecurities that threaten your identity as you take the stage.

Your Story + **Your Standards & Systems** =
Winning Your Stage

8

Performance Bubble

W ITH SECONDS LEFT IN Super Bowl XXV, the Bills were down by a single point, and it was up to kicker Scott Norwood to determine the fate of the game. It would be the only Super Bowl in history to be decided by a single point, and if Norwood succeeded in making the 47-yard kick, the Bills would win their first ever Super Bowl. 74,000 fans screamed from the stands while another 80 million watched live on television as he stepped towards the ball, kicked... and it veered **wide right**. Norwood had made countless kicks before and had missed many as well, but out of all his successes and failures, that particular kick went down in history because of the high stakes of the situation – the size of the stage.

In a striking repeat of history for Buffalo Bills fans during the 2024 playoff game against the Kansas City Chiefs, the game's destiny once again hinged on their kicker, Tyler Bass. His crucial kick, meant to equalize the AFC divisional game, unfortunately veered **wide right**! The magnitude of the stage and the weight of the game's outcome undoubtedly contributed to the intense pressure of that decisive moment.

A "stage" – whether it is a game, test, or any other evaluation of your performance – increases the pressure that you experience. Some people can adjust to the pressure while others choke. This can look like test anxiety, missing crucial free throws, or stage fright.

> **"**
> A stage creates a moment of truth because how you respond to the pressure reveals your story.
> **"**

External pressure reveals internal homeostasis. Homeostasis is the natural process of self-regulation, which keeps a person, organism, or system in balance when changes occur. It gets cold, you shiver, you warm up. It gets hot, you sweat, you cool down. When you walk onto your stage, does your nervous system spiral out of control, or are you able to slow your heart rate and execute the plan? Do you adapt to unforeseen challenges or panic? How can you ensure your internal homeostasis is prepared to handle the external pressure? The answer is not to avoid the pressure but to create a headspace where you are in absolute control—a "Performance Bubble."

Your "Performance Bubble" is a mental environment conducive to focus and freedom. It acts as a selective barrier with boundaries, welcoming elements that boost your performance and excluding those that don't. This isn't just a shield from chaos but a dynamic ecosystem nourished by the oxygen of belief in who you are. In essence, the Performance Bubble is a self-crafted zone of excellence. It's a space where your best self can emerge, unencumbered by external noise and internal doubts, allowing you to perform at your highest level.

The Performance Bubble is like an egg, symbolizing an external bubble or shell that protects the internal space where peak performance is promoted. This egg metaphor illustrates two key points:

1. Vulnerable to External Forces: Like an egg, the Performance Bubble is susceptible to external disruptions like criticism, setbacks, or distractions, which can impair focus, confidence, and performance.

2. Growth from Internal Forces: Alternatively, internal growth within the Bubble, akin to an egg hatching, represents a self-driven improvement, leading to enhanced skills and resilience, much like the emergence of new life from an egg.

In essence, the Performance Bubble's stability is crucial for peak performance, requiring protection from external negatives and nurturing through internal growth, like the care needed for an egg.

Sounds great, right? Unfortunately, this bubble is not something you can just blow up on game day.

ANCHORS AND BOUNDARIES

Building a solid Performance Bubble begins by identifying your anchors – the principles you wholeheartedly stand by and would die on a hill for, such as self-belief, confidence in your abilities, acknowledgment of your hard work and dedication, elevated standards, pre-event visualizations, and anything else vital to your success. Without these anchors, you risk drifting along with the current, leading to fluctuations in your energy, motivation, and mood based on external factors like performance outcomes and scores. On the other hand, with deliberate and premeditated anchors, you can stay centered on your dreams, goals, and mission regardless of the challenges you face.

A Performance Bubble is not a bubble unless there are boundaries and borders. Establishing these boundaries is equally as crucial as identifying anchors. Boundaries involves decisions about what you're willing to say "no" to, decisions about what or who doesn't serve your best interests, and detaching yourself from past failures, disappointments, and rejections. Failing to set these clear boundaries results in a compromised Performance Bubble that lacks integrity, structure, and effectiveness.

Building and maintaining a Performance Bubble takes intentionality, consistency, commitment, and humble confidence.

INTENTIONALITY

Many performers aren't aware or don't realize that creating a Performance Bubble is an achievable strategy. For a football player, this means establishing their Performance Bubble during the same period they're analyzing their opponent, studying their team's game plan, caring for their physical health, and gearing up for the upcoming game. Part of this process involves reflecting on past performances and fine-tuning the mental aspects of their game. This means consciously deciding what influences to allow into their mental space - if it doesn't support or benefit them, it has no place in their Bubble. Constructing this Performance Bubble is a deliberate act, one that enables them to play unencumbered, fully in the zone, and fueled by a deep-seated belief in their abilities.

CONSISTENCY

When coaches have a player of outstanding athletic ability but subpar or inconsistent performances, they'll often make comments about needing to "get the player to flip the switch." The player has the physical capabilities but can't seem to lock into their competitive, high-performance "mode" when game time comes around. The problem with this assessment is that – if a player isn't operating in this "mode" in his daily systems and practices, then the mode won't be accessible for the biggest moments.

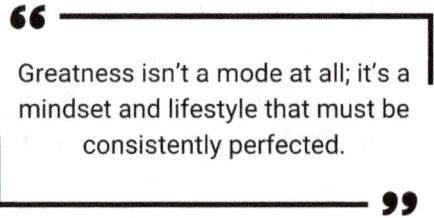

Greatness isn't a mode at all; it's a mindset and lifestyle that must be consistently perfected.

Your Performance Bubble is built over time. It begins with a strong connection with your purpose, which guides your actions and decisions. Preparation, practice, and visualization are foundational elements, all of which increase your readiness and confidence. Every time you tune into your story and turn down the noise, each time you rebuke an identity killer and choose belief instead, and every time you carry out a system at a higher standard, you are fortifying your Performance Bubble. Your Performance Bubble does not represent a "mode" it represents an intentionally crafted, heavily reinforced mindset. It is built over time to serve you when it matters most.

COMMITMENT

My senior year of high school at Maur Hill Prep in Atchison, KS, our football team began creating our Performance Bubbles before Fall camp. The team had collectively vowed to remain sober during the season as part of our commitment. This commitment reminded us of our goal: we were going to be the class to win the State Championship. Five games into the season, our commitment was paying off. We were undefeated and getting ready to face a team that hadn't yet won a game. It was also homecoming, and everybody expected us to dominate.

The Friday night before the Saturday afternoon homecoming game, there was a big bonfire, and everybody went. Overconfident about the next day's game and forgetting our priorities, almost all the football players abandoned our commitment and drank alcohol.

The next day, we found ourselves behind 14-0 going into the fourth quarter. I remember having a conversation with God at the end of the third quarter, confessing that this wasn't the plan, asking for his supernatural power, and acknowledging our inability to turn the game around without His help. (God doesn't really care who wins, but there are always moments when you need more than you. Leave room for this in your Performance Bubble). Thankfully, we went into overtime, won the game, went undefeated, and accomplished our goal of winning state, but our lapse in commitment almost cost us greatly.

We'd been building our Performance Bubble all season by holding ourselves to a higher standard in what we put into our bodies. This commitment reinforced our purpose, motivated us to work hard, and even united our Pit Crew (each other) around a common goal. When we made an exception to our standard and thought we could just "flip the switch" for an easy game, we contaminated the Performance Bubble we'd been building.

Pro Tip

The truth is, there is no exception to what decisions affect your Performance Bubble; every thought and action either builds or corrupts it.

" Learning to commit to big and small stages with the same level of confidence and importance is the key to building a lasting bubble that won't be affected by high pressure situations. "

Imagine a balance beam one foot off the ground; how confidently could you walk across it? Now, put that same balance beam across a 500-foot gorge. Has the challenge increased? No, but the stakes and danger certainly have. To cross the 500-foot gorge with the confidence of walking on the foot-high beam, you must first treat your practice – walking on the foot-high beam – with as much importance as you would walking the beam 500 feet in the air. In the same way, committing to each rep as if it's as important as the Super Bowl-winning point will help you to treat the Super Bowl-winning point with as much confidence as if it's just another practice rep. If my senior year football team had treated our Homecoming Game with as much importance as if it were the State Championship, we wouldn't have felt overconfident, and we wouldn't have found ourselves in that nail-biting situation.

HUMBLE CONFIDENCE

Pride and complacency can hinder the creation of your Performance Bubble. It's not uncommon to see a first round Draft pick crumble under pressure. Name, Image, and Likeness (NIL) dollars, pampering, and extensive publicity are usually given to first rounders before they've even made it to the League. They are treated as if they've already crossed the gorge on the 500-foot-high beam before they've even crossed the foot-high beam. In essence, they are given the impression of assured success in the League as first-round draft picks, even before they have truly proven themselves and secured their spot on the team. Meanwhile, late-rounders and undrafted free agent players are grinding just for a chance to prove themselves. Every day has been their stage, so when they make the team, they understand that every day is still their stage. They must stay in the grind and continue to earn their spot day in and day out. The pressure of earning and then keeping their job is constant – so they build up resilience against the pressure. There is no "switch" to flip. Their only mode is 100% effort, and their switch is always "on." They operate at full speed in a perpetual Performance Bubble.

Comparatively, some first rounders can become overconfident and therefore complacent. Assured that their place on the team is secure, they may fail to build a Performance Bubble in the first place. They may begin to rely on external validation for their confidence such as the media narrative and hefty signing bonuses, but when the season starts, draft status doesn't save anyone who fails to perform. If they didn't truly put in the work to prepare, they're unable to hold this elevated identity. They've believed the media's story of their greatness, but they haven't aligned their actions to match it. Meanwhile, a late rounder/free agent has been tuning out the naysayers and writing his own story. Each day in practice, his full effort reinforces his story of greatness and builds his Performance Bubble.

An elevated identity fueled by pride leads to complacency. On the other hand, any self-doubt will be magnified under pressure, so it must be eradicated from your Performance Bubble. Ryan Porter, former pro quarterback and current QB coach, knew how to hold these two forces of belief and humility in balance. He was once the skinny kid, 7th on the depth chart, but he was eventually given the opportunity to see the stage. His coaches knew they could count on him to show up when they asked him to show up, because he was the guy to do the right things when no one was looking. Being committed to the process even when there is no audience prepares you for when there is an audience. "When you train, I have the mindset that everybody is better than me who's training. If I'm not up early, there's somebody up earlier working harder than me. But when it's time to compete and it's game day," Coach Porter explained, "There's nobody in the country on that field that's better than me." This mindset motivated him to consistently hit the highest standard, which built his Performance Bubble. In turn, self-doubt didn't stand a chance once he took the stage. His confidence was earned through repetition and successful execution (his systems), which bolstered his already steadfast belief in himself (his story).

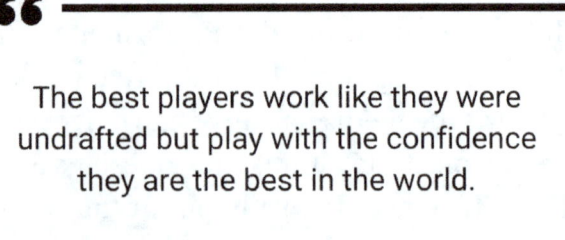

The best players work like they were undrafted but play with the confidence they are the best in the world.

GAME DAY

Though building a Performance Bubble happens over the course of your preparation, when it's time to take your stage, stepping into that Performance Bubble requires real-time courage and mental management. Rituals, breathing, process-oriented, and a positive pocket voice can help you maintain the homeostasis of your Bubble.

Rituals help recenter athletes within their bubble. Dribbling the ball the same number of times before shooting a free throw, listening to a certain playlist before running out on the field, and even putting on the same pair of game day underwear are all examples of superficial rituals that can help the mind return to its mental sanctuary. These rituals provide a sense of comfort in an uncomfortable situation. By doing the same routine, players remember all the previous successes and practice shots, which helps them to regard the stage with the same amount of pressure. In other words, rituals can help you walk the 500-foot balance beam with as much confidence as all the times you walked the foot-high beam.

One universally beneficial ritual is conscious breathing. The stress of a stage can cause your body to enter fight or flight mode. Your peripheral vision narrows, and you feel as though you're losing control. Your heart rate increases followed by anxiety. Deep breaths are profoundly impactful in stressful situations. When doubt whispers in your ear and your body tells you to breathe quick, shallow breaths, taking a deep, slow breath allows you to reclaim authority over your body, your Performance Bubble, and your stage. It not only physiologically signals your body to relax, but it also boosts your confidence.

What is the oxygen you breathe in your Performance Bubble? The oxygen should be "belief."

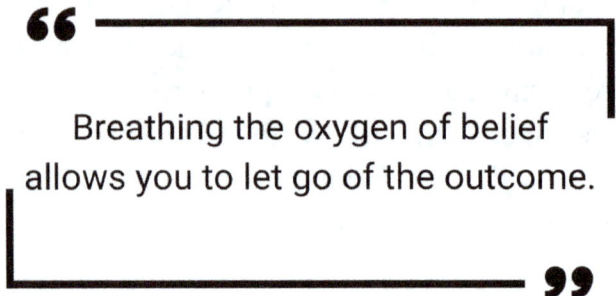

Breathing the oxygen of belief allows you to let go of the outcome.

When the pressure gets to you, you might think, "This has to work," which invites the fear of failure into your mental sanctuary. When a quarterback worries about the outcome of his throw, his hand grips the ball just a little bit more. This tighter grip sends tension up the rest of his arm, which affects his entire throwing mechanics, and the ball ends up at his receiver's feet. If he took a deep breath and simply believed in his process instead of stressing about the outcome, he could throw freely, trusting that all his preparation would take care of the outcome.

Nevertheless, there are bound to be surprises on stage. Regardless of your preparation, mistakes will be made, and unexpected situations will arise. The strength of your Performance Bubble depends on how you respond to these challenges. Suppose building your Performance Bubble involves shutting out negativity from a certain family member, and then that family member shows up on game day. Can you focus on the game, or will the distraction infiltrate your bubble? What about intangible distractions? Imagine that you're giving a well-rehearsed speech and suddenly, you remember a point you forgot to add. Can you weave it in seamlessly, or will the thought throw you off and cause you to stammer?

Your bubble must have an "escape hatch" where you can kick out unsolicited thoughts, doubts, and distractions and replace them with positive affirmations. Take in another deep breath of belief. Ask yourself what is true? Connect to the deeper truth of your worth, your story, and your purpose. Remind yourself the outcome does not measure your worthiness. If your pocket voice says, "You're failing; you look like an idiot," do not respond to chaos with chaos by telling yourself, "Shut the *&%# up!" Instead, tap into your greater purpose and allow the escape hatch to be a channel for bringing in positive affirmations and moving out negative thoughts.

> **"**
> Your Performance Bubble is a
> sacred mental space where you
> can be your authentic and best self.
> **"**

It's an adaptable ecosystem that maintains internal homeostasis regardless of external circumstances. Whether you are walking the balance beam a foot off the ground or 500 feet in the air, your bubble – built by higher-standard systems of training and filled with the oxygen of belief – will allow you to remain calm, focus on your process, and perform your best.

CHAPTER 8 RECAP

1. External pressure reveals internal homeostasis.

2. A Performance Bubble helps you maintain homeostasis and perform freely and perform your best.

3. The fundamental process is identifying anchors and boundaries.

4. Building a Performance Bubble takes consistency, commitment, and humble confidence.

- Performing at a high level isn't a "mode" you can switch on and off; it is a mindset of consistent greatness.

- Your Performance Bubble is built through a commitment to higher standards.

- Neither pride nor doubt are conducive to building an effective Performance Bubble.

5. Recentering within your Performance Bubble on stage is aided by rituals, breathing, processes, and positive self-talk.

- Rituals provide comfort and help us regard the stage with as much confidence as our training systems.

- Controlled breathing regulates our stress response; belief is the oxygen.

- Don't hyper-focus on the outcomes; instead, believe fully in your process.

- Install an escape hatch for unsolicited thoughts, doubts, and distractions.

6. Remember the Egg Metaphor - the Performance Bubble is susceptible to external disruptions like criticism, setbacks, or distractions, which can impair focus, confidence, and performance. Alternatively, internal growth represents a self-driven improvement, leading to enhanced skills and resilience, much like the emergence of new life from an egg.

9

Be In the Moment

"It's not the number of hours you practice. It's about the number of hours your mind is present during practice." Kobe Bryant.

ICE BOWL: THE ESSENCE OF TRUE PRESENCE

I WANT TO RECOUNT a story that embodies the essence of truly "showing up," both in body and spirit. This took place during my tenure as a youth football coach on a Saturday morning characterized by icy, bone-chilling conditions in Colorado Springs. Our journey to the south side of the city for the game was treacherous, riddled with black ice. Given the extreme cold, a challenging game lay ahead, especially for 6th graders unaccustomed to such weather and one 5th grader.

Our team featured two quarterbacks. The starting quarterback was exceptionally talented and a future Division I baseball pitcher. My son, Brock, the lone 5th grader, played as the backup quarterback. A year younger and playing in a higher age group to avoid me coaching two separate teams, Brock often felt the sting of not playing, though it was clear the starter was older, a good leader, and had a stronger arm.

Brock (#19) and JoJo (#7) at picture day for their first tackle football season.

Upon reaching the field, the weather had worsened, complicating matters. Our starter hadn't brought gloves, unlike Brock, who had packed receiver gloves for warmth and grip. During warm-ups, the starter's fingers froze, leading him to retreat to his dad's truck to warm up.

This unforeseen circumstance propelled Brock into the starting role. Faced with horrible weather, we could have opted for simple run plays, but we chose to stick with our pass-first strategy. Brock stepped up, throwing with a precision that belied the frigid conditions. We caught the opposing team off guard and won a significant victory.

As a younger player, Brock was fully present. He was too young to think about expectations, outcomes or the past but was locked into the moment and the execution of each play call. This game marked the start of Brock's journey as a quarterback, handling the role of a starting QB with poise. From that point on, we alternated between the two QBs, as Brock had earned his spot and the respect of his teammates.

The lesson from this Ice Bowl moment goes beyond football. Brock's success in this game was a personal victory that taught him that being prepared and locked into the moment is the key to winning his stage.

FOOTBALL ON THE BRAIN

As a young teenager, my client Rob Ninkovich, began writing down his goals. "Make it to the NFL" was among the most prominent. Having limited opportunities out of high school, Rob worked part-time in a steel factory while playing football at a junior college. He continued to believe in himself and work hard with football on the brain. "If you don't ever give up on something, you have the belief that you can do it, and you put in the effort to get it done, then your chances of being successful are very high." Rob accepted a scholarship to Purdue University, where he continued his football career. He was drafted in the fifth round of the 2006 NFL Draft by the New Orleans Saints.

In an end of the season exit, the Miami Dolphins' head coach bluntly told him he didn't fit the NFL. The next three years were a roller coaster ride between rehab, active rosters, and practice squads. Rob was let go five times in the first 22 months of his career. When he was back with the Saints, Head Coach Sean Payton told Rob his only chance to make the roster was as a long snapper, but he continued to train as if he would play defense. Rob remembers, "This guy can't be serious. That's all he thinks I have." Coach Payton then waived Rob the first day of training camp. How would you respond to such disappointment?

A few days later, Rob faced a crucial workout opportunity. Flying overnight to Boston, he arrived sleep-deprived for a workout with the Patriots. Despite the odds, he excelled and secured a one-year contract. Later that day at his first practice,

Rob, an unknown player at the time, stunned everyone by beating Pro Bowler Matt Light in one-on-one drills, not just once but three times using different pass rush moves. This day marked a significant shift in Rob's career, as the Patriots began to recognize his true potential. From that day, the Patriots saw him as he saw himself. On September 10, 2010, Rob earned his first start of his NFL career and went on to start 117 games in his NFL career.

Rob was a warrior for the Patriots during the 2010-15 seasons, playing in every game. During his eight seasons, he made numerous key plays, he recorded 52 sacks, 518 tackles, and numerous key plays (forced fumbles, fumbles recovered, interceptions, sacks, and tackles for loss). When asked about his mindset, he puts it simply: "Maximize my God-given talents," and "Be the best football player I can possibly be."

When the Patriots played the Giants in the 2012 Super Bowl, Rob looked up at the scoreboard, saw they were ahead, and thought, "We're going to win." They lost.

Three years later on Rob's birthday, he had another chance at a Super Bowl victory against the Seattle Seahawks. Head Coach Belichick offered some wisdom before the game: "If you start to think about the outcome of the game, get yourself back to the moment" and simply "win your down." This time, Rob didn't look at the scoreboard, but stayed focused on the guy across from him. Rob explains, "When you start to think about the outcome of things before the job is done, that's when things start to go the wrong way," but if everyone just does the job in front of them, everything takes care of itself.

As a five-time defensive captain, Rob retired after a second Super Bowl win against the Falcons in 2017, capping a remarkable career.

Looking back, he sees that he was always meant to go to New Orleans and find his wife, to get injured and experience the trials and tribulations, and to learn that "it's the strength you carry on through those obstacles that makes or breaks [who] you are as a person." If he'd focused too much on the past – all the times he was discouraged, dismissed, and rejected – or too much on the future – wondering what would happen if his next opportunity flopped – he never would have been able to fully seize the moment that changed his entire career.

Life is full of ups and downs. We can't change the past, and we can't predict the future. But, when we can focus on the role, the job, the rep, the down, the moment in front of us, and give it our best self, remarkable things unfold. Rob wrote down his big goals, but he also wrote down countless others. All of the smaller goals for today led him to the big goals of tomorrow.

Rob and I after a AFC Championship game in Foxborough.

> "Most humans are never fully present in the now because they unconsciously believe the next moment must be more important than this one. But then you miss your whole life, which is never not now." —Eckhart Tolle.

"Most humans are never fully present in the now because they unconsciously believe the next moment must be more important than this one. But then you miss your whole life, which is never not now." —Eckhart Tolle.

Rob is an example of what it takes to be great: Seeing each moment as an opportunity and embracing it with his full belief and best effort. It's as simple and as extraordinarily complex as that.

Life changes constantly, and therefore, your Pro Mindset must adjust accordingly. You'll never stop adjusting because life will never be static. You tune things out, turn things down, invent new things, add things to your repertoire, and try new systems. You go perform, you succeed, or you don't, and just when you think you have something calibrated perfectly -- something goes awry -- and it's time to adjust again. Your story, purpose, and identity are the foundation of Pro Mindset, but being fully present is the key to unlocking anything built upon this foundation.

When former NFL offensive line coach Bob Wylie accompanied me to a youth practice, he taught the kids this same, invaluable lesson. When the kids made a big mistake, Bob walked into the huddle. "Do you know what you do right now guys?" he asked as the kids looked up at him, in awe of his reputation and ready for whatever bit of professional level wisdom he had to offer. "Flush it," he said. "That play's over. Just flush it. Let's move on." Bob's simple statement was impactful. On the Ted Lasso show, the coach told his players to be goldfish because goldfish are said to have a 10-second memory. The message is to move on from mistakes rather than lingering on them. The past is just a former limitation. It doesn't matter if it's been 10 years or 10 seconds, the past does not define your story. Learn from it if you can. Reframe it if you have the time. But most importantly, flush it, and move on. Focus on the next play.

Being present means being grateful for where your feet are. If you are dwelling on the referee's call, you'll miss the next play. If you are too focused on getting a new contract, your full self won't even show up to practice. But if you gratefully live in the moment, you are given now, you can seize it to the best of your ability. And if you have visualized this moment, that's even more reason to experience each snap, each step, and each breath when it happens.

I used to fly out to see clients only to spend the trip missing my family back home. Then when I was home, my mind would wander away from the dinner table and linger on work. I was rarely where my feet were.

> **Trust the process. God has a plan for everybody.**

The advice Rob Ninkovich would give his younger self rings true for me too: "Trust the process. God has a plan for everybody."

My daughter Rylee is an artist and performer at heart. When she was in high school, she was always one of the leads in plays and musicals, which was fun, but the arts were never my thing. I played sports. Still, I wanted to support her as a dad and went to just one show of each of her plays. Sure, my phone was on, but the light was dimmed so nobody knew if I made a work text. The truth was, I was never fully present.

During the play Grease, Rylee played Sandy. As she performed one of her solos, "Hopelessly Devoted to You," I watched her let go and fully embody the persona of Sandra Dee. I saw her, in real time, be great. I saw her perform in a manner consistent with who God created her to be. She was in her Performance Bubble, free from any chains of doubt. She had the entire audience and cast in her palm. Hearts were touched, activated, and entertained.

I've watched thousands of football, basketball, and soccer games, and I've never cried. But sitting in that theater, witnessing in real time as my daughter dropped into her confidence and brought the house down, I felt everything that she was, and I cried. It was awesome.

Rylee performing in Grease.

I'd only ever been to one show of a single play before, but they actually do those things multiple times! Teddi, being the super mom, never missed one, but some dads are slow learners. I had an epiphany after Rylee's performance in Grease, that theater is a lot like a football game, no two are ever the same even if you play the same team. When I went to Rylee's second show that weekend, it was a totally different experience! Because she's not a robot, she interacted and responded to her other cast members in a unique way. I ended up going three times, and each time, I experienced different details. I realized what I had been missing all along. By not being fully present, I'd been robbing myself of seeing my daughter absolutely shine. I missed the details and was totally oblivious to the opportunity in front of me to not only see it again, but to experience it differently the next time.

No two moments are the same. So let go of the last performance. Forget about the audience. Don't fret so much about the outcome, and just take the stage and BE your best.

> " Don't fret so much about the outcome, and just take the stage and BE your best. "

10

Pro Mindset: ReThink Your Reality

NAVIGATING THE TWISTS AND turns of life's journey is akin to an unpredictable and exhilarating game, one that requires us to constantly recalibrate, adjust, and innovate our strategies. In this game of life, we are the players with the power to decide how we engage in each unfolding moment, and whether we fully immerse ourselves in the present experience.

We have the option to linger in the memories of our former selves, to replay our previous victories and defeats. We might fixate on our doubters and critics, giving energy to those who didn't or don't believe in us. Our minds can wander into the realm of the future, filled with fantasies, worries, and the illusion of control. The choice of succumbing to fears, like the fear of failure or rejection, is always present.

However, we also have the empowering option to embrace gratitude, recognizing each moment as a priceless chance to author our own narrative, adhere to our personal standards, and excel on our own stage. By choosing this path, we see beyond the transient challenges and focus on the opportunity each moment brings to create, perform, and triumph.

It's about understanding that life, much like the competitive world of sports, is not just about reacting to what's thrown at us, but about proactively shaping our journey with intention, resilience, and an unwavering belief in our worth. This is the essence of living with a Pro Mindset, where we transform every experience into an opportunity to demonstrate our worth, grow from our gap, and celebrate our unique journey on the stage of life.

WHAT'S THE STORY YOU'RE TELLING YOURSELF?

Connect with your current self.

Are you stuck in the narrative of your past?

Are you influenced by external doubters and your own inner skeptic?

Are you mastering your internal conversation, aligning with your inner voice, and opting for self-belief?

Are you fully embracing your worth?

Today, regardless of your situation, are you committing to absolute 100% self-belief?

Are you willing to confront what's truly hindering your progress?

Continuously reclaim and rewrite your story, as many times as necessary. The most powerful action is to craft a new narrative.

WHAT IS YOUR GAP?

Face the reality of your situation head-on. Don't shy away from it, conceal it, or be untruthful about it.

The gap should not be overlooked, denied, or avoided; instead, view it as an avenue for **G**rowth, **A**dvancement, and **P**rogress.

Acknowledge your Gap and then reshape the narrative around it. See it not as a barrier but as an invitation to construct your bridge to cross it.

The Gap you faced yesterday might differ from the Gap you'll encounter tomorrow, but a gap will always exist. There's always room for growth and new dreams to pursue.

Embrace your Gap wholeheartedly.

Be truthful with yourself about your Gap.

Recognize and appreciate the unique potential of your Gap.

Now is the time to actively attack your Gap!

WHAT STANDARDS & SYSTEMS ARE YOU WORKING TO GET THERE?

Whether you're kickstarting your day, working out, earning a living, or spending time with friends, remember that our systems are constantly evolving, and each is important. Every moment presents a chance to enhance, innovate, and go the extra mile, upholding a higher standard in all that you do.

Maintaining a higher standard is easier said than done.

Approach your next task, no matter how ordinary, with the utmost standard. Execute it with excellence. Bring intentionality, energy, and focus to even the simplest of actions.

Strive for systems that are straightforward yet precise. The way you handle one task often sets the tone for everything else. Engage in thorough preparation and practice. Approach each action with the respect and attention it merits, rather than just mechanically going through the motions.

Focus on visualizing success as the result of your

efforts. Avoid getting hung up on the worst-case scenarios. Take control of the narratives and movies you create in your mind, choosing to envision the most favorable outcomes. Embracing success in your mental rehearsals is crucial before manifesting it in reality. Although success may occasionally occur unexpectedly, why leave it to chance?

Seeing your success in your mind's eye first can make a significant difference. It's not just about visualizing but believing in the possibility of victory. This belief is a game-changer and can be the deciding factor in whether you triumph on your personal and professional stages.

ARE YOU WINNING YOUR STAGE?

Your stage. What is your stage? Define it. Are you showing up as your full, authentic self and standing in all your worth? Are you waiting until later to "find" your Performance Bubble, allowing insecurities and identity killers to infiltrate it, or are you using right *NOW* to build it with intention, consistency, commitment, and humble confidence?

Recognize that your stage is *now*. *Now* is your time to shine. *Now* is the moment you've been preparing for. *Now* is the pivotal space where big opportunities and crucial moments unfold. Win your stage by winning the *now*.

Don't hesitate! Don't overthink! Stop waiting until the next moment to exercise your Pro Mindset. Act Now. Apply it to the now. If you continue to do so, you will transcend both your former limitations and your most fantastic dreams.

CHALLENGE

> **"** I challenge you to rewrite your story, work your systems and win on your stage. It all starts with finding your purpose. **"**

Thank you for reading Pro Mindset! I challenge you to rewrite your story, work your systems and win on your stage. It all starts with finding your purpose. You are a unique and marvelous creation, unparalleled in this world, with no one before you or after you quite like you. Our most profound purpose is to embrace the gifts, talents, passion, and calling that God has placed on our lives. As our Creator, He invites you to leave a meaningful imprint on the world. Release any constraints, free yourself from any limitations, and fully embody what God intended you to be. If others disapprove, let not their opinions hinder you. Embrace your true self as crafted by God. The key to realizing this lies in deepening your relationship with Him, allowing Him to unveil your path and walk alongside you.

Be your best in your biggest moments. Adopt a Pro Mindset today!

I'm working on Craig 3.0!

YOUR NEXT CHAPTER STARTS NOW...

To get your **free book bonuses,** you may go to this link: https://www.craigdomann.com/book-bonuses or scan the QR code below:

Index

Alphabetical Order by Last Name

Paul Alexander, page 89

Muhammed Ali, page 16, 36

Roger Bannister, page 15

Marion Barber III, page 19

Tiki Barber, page 86

Tyler Bass, page 93

Martha Beck, page 58

Tom Brady, page 9, 13, 78

George Brett, page 37

Kobe Bryant, page 106

Cam Cameron, page 108

Chris Chester, pages 88, 89

Lavonte David, page 51

David Diehl, pages 85, 86, 87

Brock Domann, pages iii, vi, ix, xii, xvi, 37, 39, 64, 70, 71, 72, 73, 90, 107, 108

JoJo Domann, pages iii, iv, vi, 26, 29, 37, 39, 71, 107

Rylee Domann, pages iii, vi, ix, xii, xv, 33, 68, 69, 75, 112, 113

Teddi Domann, pages iii, xi, 31, 39, 56, 69, 90, 113

Martha Goedert, page 25

Brock Gutierrez, page 90, 91

Jesus, page 66

Michael Jordan, page 59

Peter King, page 9

Chris Kuper, page 60

Ted Lasso, page 111

Mike Lehan, page 79

Matt Light, page 109

Ryan Lilja, page 74, 75

Eli Manning, pages xi, 86

Peyton Manning, page xi

Tom Nalen, page 60

Rob Ninkovich, pages 108, 109, 110, 111, 112

Scott Norwood, page 93

Laura Okmin, pages 76, 77, 78

Terrell Owens, page 19

Sean Payton, page 108

Lou Pinella, page 42

Ryan Porter, page 101

Duke Preston, pages 27, 29, 51

Luke Rhodes, page viii, 53

Tony Robbins, page 61

Drew Rosenhaus, page 20

Greg Scruggs, page 5

Jeremy Shockey, page 86

Bill Snyder, page 74, 75

Michael Strahan, page 86

Ndamukong Suh, page 51

Bob Tewksbury, pages 42

Nick Tiano, page 51

Eckhart Tolle, page 111

Anthony Trucks, page v

Dick Vermeil, page 75

Adam Vinatieri, page 53

Lydia Weatherford, page iv

Sterling Weatherford, page iv, 23, 24, 25, 26

Ken Whisenhunt, page 59

Bob Wylie, page 111

Alphabetical Order by Team or School

Arizona Cardinals, page 59

Atlanta Falcons, page 110

Buffalo Bills, page 93

Campbell University, page 71

Cincinnati Bengals, page 89

Dallas Cowboys, page 19

Denver Broncos, page 60

Dresden Monarchs, page ix, xii, xvi

IMG Academy, page 79

Independence Community College, page 71

Indianapolis Colts, pages iv, viii, 23, 24, 26, 53, 74, 75, 90

Kansas City Chiefs, pages 75, 93

Kansas City Royals, page 37

Kansas State University, page 74

Maur Hill Preparatory School, page 98

Miami Dolphins, page 108

Minnesota Vikings, page viii, 60

New England Patriots, pages 42, 109

New Orleans Saints, pages 79, 108

New York Giants, page 85, 86, 109

New York Yankees, page 42

Pine Creek High School, pages x, 38, 39, 84
Purdue University, page 108
San Diego Chargers, page 50
Seattle Seahawks, page 109
Tampa Bay Buccaneers, pages 9, 27, 51
Tennessee Titans, page xvi, 74
University of Louisville, pages ix, 40, 41, 72
University of Nebraska, pages vii, 67, 73
University of North Dakota, page 60
University of Oklahoma, page 88
University of Virginia, page 40
Ventura Community College, page 71

Alphabetical Order by Organization or Company:

4-H, page 90
American Ninja Warriors, page v
German Football League (GFL), page ix
Miss Rodeo America, page 90
Miss Rodeo Kansas, page 90
McDonald's Corporation, page 90
McDonald's All-American High School Basketball
Game, page 90
National Football League (NFL), pages iii, vii, viii, xi,
xiii, xiv, 1, 2, 3, 4, 5, 6, 11, 29, 41, 47, 50, 52, 53, 59, 60,
63, 66, 67, 75, 76, 79
National Hot Rod Association (NHRA), page 90
United States Olympic Committee, page 90
World Cup, page 90